"In the pursuit of spiritual attainment, it is easier with help. If a baby holds its father's hand the baby can still stubble and fall, if the father holds the baby's hand the likelihood of the baby falling is small."

— Unknown

"Watch your thoughts, they become your words; watch your words, they become your actions; watch your actions, they become your habits; watch your habits, they become your character; watch your character, it becomes your destiny."

— Lao Tzu

Table of Contents

PREFACE

This book does not follow any specific religious premise or belief. Instead, it invites readers to turn inward, diving deep within to explore the Self, the truth which all should be in search of! his text was written with the hope of showing readers that they are fully capable of connecting with their inner Self and source energy—what many may call a Higher Power or God—whenever one is ready!

Within this book, you will encounter two variations of the word *you*. The lowercase you refers to the self as the physical body—the part of you that exists in a lower vibration and perceives the world through the senses, the realm of the seen. The capitalized *You* represents the Inner Self, or True Self, which is directly connected to Source—the essence from which all things arise—the unseen.

Upon starting this writing, I was VERY angry with God! I was angry with this all-powerful, omnipresent, *all-this and all-that* being who allowed someone close to me to die. This person was not perfect by any means, but was perfect for and to me. They were a foundational and intricate piece to all parts of my life and shaped me into the person I am today. The death of my mom is not why I was angry, how she died—how she suffered—is!

For most of my life—and even presently—I pray to God, to this entity that is said to be in the heavenly sky. And I would wait for responses that seemed to never come. Yet, as I look back on the course of my life, most situations, requests, and needs that I prayed about were in one way or another resolved at some point.

During times of prayer, I was of the utmost belief that I was in talks with God. What I mean by God is some big guy who looks down from the sky with all his power— the creator of the universe with billions of galaxies, trillions of planets and stars, Earth, and little ole me.

He was in talks with *me*! "Is this even possible," I asked myself. "Of course, anything is possible," my optimistic self replies! Then, just like those old school cartoons, a devil appears on my shoulder. He—my pessimistic self—then asks, "Or is it that am I talking with myself and having this conversation in my own head?" Oh, crap—I look around frantically—am I going crazy? Now, a cascade of questions is unleashed. What or who is this voice that I hear inside of Me? Am I referring to myself as the innate essence or the spirit of what we call God, or is there another entity—perhaps the evolving wisdom of the mind—engaged in dialogue? Then, naturally, the question arises—who or what is *myself*? In what way do I know Me that is my Self? So, I just asked God! Let's see what is unraveled!

Awake sleeping soul, awake to the unsleeping, unchanging Self, awake that which I know as me, awake this consciousness that knows all!

Chapter One: Conversations with the Divine

Me: Hey God, for a good while I was extremely unhappy and angry with You at the passing of my mother. The anger was not with her death, as I know we all must die, but more in how she died! I saw so much pain, so much agony, torment, suffering, and even her fear of death as she told me she did not want to die. It was not easy to hear the howling shrieks of her voice calling my name for help, for relief and comfort of her pain. Still to this day, it gives me chills to remember the horrendous howl of her voice, which sickened my body in the worst of ways as I was powerless to help her! My question is what is one to learn from such suffering or in a situation as this?

God: My son, there is much to learn—or rather, to experience—in this life you are living. Suffering and pain are much like a sword: in one moment it can protect, and in another it can wound, bringing harm and even death. The pain and suffering you speak of are never easy, and they are often unwanted. Yet, within them lies an invitation to recognize the many layers and interactions of life—to see its totality. You must learn to immerse your Self fully in life, to live joyfully, freely, and with gratitude while breath is still within you. The feelings you describe reflect your deep love and empathy for others, which at times causes you to carry what they are going through. This suffering, though difficult, is a necessary part of growth. It is shaping and preparing you for the journey ahead—teaching you the ways of life as you walk the path between birth and death as you now know it.

Me: It just hit me, why is it that I can hear you so clearly now? After many years of constant conversations and prayers, what makes it possible to hear You, now?

God: Simple—you finally chose to listen with an open heart and mind. A better question might be: why was it so easy for you to ignore Me? Think of it like a phone receiving upgrades to improve its operating system. The human spirit works the same way. Growth can happen naturally, or when one chooses it. But these inner upgrades can become blocked or distorted by many things— environment, poor nourishment, negativity, and harmful words, to name a few. I have been guiding you quietly in the background, though often unnoticed. This shows that there is still more inner work for you to do.

Me: How does one get through the pain of a loss like this?

God: Any loss rooted in a loving connection and deep bond can feel overwhelming, though its intensity varies from person to person. When faced with loss, our natural instinct is to search for what is no longer there. Yet death is not truly a loss—it is a transition to another energetic state or realm. Death is also a constant. Everything in the material world comes to an end—everybody, every season, every form. This truth, while painful, also gives life its depth and urgency. For if all things remained unchanged, would we ever treasure them? It is the very recognition of death that breathes meaning into life, calling us to ask: *How should I live? What truly matters? Whom shall I love while I can?* In these moments, give yourself permission to grieve fully. Healing does not follow a

straight line, and there is no "right way" or "right time" to move through pain. Grief may come in waves— sometimes heavy, sometimes light—and that is natural. At the same time, remember that love does not die. The bond you shared is not broken but transformed. Look for your beloved in the small reminders, in memories that suddenly surface, in the quiet presence that lingers in your heart.

Allow joy, peace, and glimpses of happiness when they appear, without guilt. Do not add to your pain by clinging to suffering; instead, allow your mind and body the space they need to grieve and heal naturally. And through it all, I invite you to turn to Me—to listen for My voice in the midst of the chaos and sorrow. Know that I am always here, speaking softly in the quiet whispers of your soul.

I am the source of comfort in the storm. Quiet your mind, and truly listen, for in Me, you will find the fulfillment of your deepest yearnings in ways beyond comprehension.

Me: What does it mean to *quiet or still your mind*? That sounds like some monk stuff!

God: Think of the mind as a raging river after a downpour—it is very hard for anything to cross without peril. Now, think of a river that is low and gently moving, or maybe it has a dam—the water is quiet and still, the water is safe. Similarly, the mind can be likened to these contrasting states. To begin, seek out a tranquil environment devoid of distractions, for the mind generates enough noise on its own. Settle into a comfortable yet alert posture, finding a balance between relaxation and attentiveness. Next, do what comes naturally—breathe! Direct your attention to the natural rhythm of your breath—inhaling slowly, exhaling gently.

Notice the sensation of air passing through your nostrils and exiting your mouth. As you do so, allow your stomach to relax, attuning yourself to its rhythmic movement. Fully immerse yourself in the present moment, letting your body unwind completely. With your intention firmly set on acquiring knowledge, maintain your focus on the breath, cultivating patience and steadiness as you delve deeper into your quest.

Me: Could You please share how one might avoid bringing about suffering?

God: In one's life there are many interactions and many dynamic happenings that cannot be controlled. However, what can be controlled is one's own life—the mind, the life forces of the body, and what comes into the body. With this in mind, suffering can be understood as trauma in the form of pain (physical or mental) or adversity that is consistent for some time and seems without end. Suffering comes in many forms: diseases of

9

the body, negative talk from yourself and others, the ability to not to allow change, an uneasiness of the mind or lack of control of the mind, any negative situation that is cyclic in nature, and injury are just some of these forms. For example, one may have a terminal illness or cancer that brings them immense pain—this suffering is of the physical body. One may reflect on the past and find happenings or situations they wish they could change or rectify—this tends to cause suffering of the mind. It is one thing to remember or bring about an old memory, however trying to relive a memory as the present will create chaos in the mind, setting off an avalanche that will be hard to stop or dig one's way out from under. In short, suffering is the ability to allow a trauma to continuously dictate the outcome of one's life in a negative manner. No matter the state of one's present situation, one has the power and authority to control how they respond or act in relation to that situation or trauma. The path forward is simple (but not always easy). Remain calm, patient, and positive. Breathe with intention, hold the desired outcome clearly in your mind, and continue to see, feel, and trust it— taking steady, purposeful action until the goal is fulfilled.

Me: Hey God, what tends to be on your mind?

God: (Jolly laugh) Everything!

Me: How do you handle everything being on your mind?

God: As everything is, I am! Just as life happens, I am always happening, always present, and always conscious! I am the experiencer and observer in all that is! There is nothing to handle, as I AM, everything just IS! I created all things and beings with the intent that each may live life to the fullest—allowing what is natural, cosmic, and divine to unfold exactly as it is meant to be.

There is nothing to manage, for I Am, and everything simply exists as it should.

Me: In life, it seems most people choose a path that straddles both good and bad. Is it natural to be good or is it natural to be bad?

God: Neither. What one sees as "good" and "bad" are but mere dualities of each other, two sides of the same coin. When individuals perceive life through this dualistic lens, their actions, thoughts, and outlook tend to waver between these extremes. Both are inherent within me— they serve as influencers of the flesh or reflections of one's authentic spirit. Life should not be limited to this narrow view of "good" or "bad." Consider the shark that eats the fish—is it inherently "bad"?

Life transcends the limitations of "good" or "bad" labels; much like the shark's nature to eat the fish, it is not about assigning moral judgment. Instead, the focus should be on personal growth and contributing positively to the world. What matters is how one acts and the impact on oneself and others. However, the choice and its consequences are always within your fingertips of influence. So, the choice is yours, as is the outcome!

Me: Ok, so what about that person or people who just kill or steal for pleasure? Or the millions of other unscrupulous things people drum up in their mind. Are there consequences?

God: Is there not a consequence dealt by your judicial system? Whether it is penance, a fine, jail time, a beating, or death—are those not consequential enough? What seems to you as good versus bad, right versus wrong seems to change to suit the person. A person murdered by a criminal is mourned by their mother just as the criminal who gets death for their deed is mourned by theirs. What is *right* and what is *wrong*?

Me: So, what happens to these so-called bad people then?

God: Did you not play God by becoming judge and jury?

Me: Ok, so what happens to those who get away with horrific crimes? What do You do?

God: There are universal fail safes within the construct of life and within each one's personal ledger—a karmic debt that will be paid in full.

Me: I am not sure what to say next!

Me: So, what advice would you give to one in this short life we live?!

God: Simple, any life not fully immersed in the art and act of living is one step closer to death! Life is a gift meant to be lived fully! Life is everywhere—in you, around you, and through you. The choice is yours in how you want to experience it, but experience is the key to a life lived and a life fulfilled!

Me: How does one immerse themselves in life?

God: To truly immerse yourself in life, you must awaken to the awareness of it within and around you. See yourself reflected in all things, and recognize the essence that connects you to everything. Do not settle for merely existing—dive fully into the experience, as if it were the only life, you will ever live... Embrace it with presence, gratitude, and wholehearted courage.

Delve into the exploration of the world surrounding you and the profound depths within. Recognize that this life is the sole one bestowed upon you. One way to immerse oneself in life is by actively engaging with experiences, people, and opportunities. It involves being present in the moment, embracing new challenges, exploring passions, and continuously learning. To immerse oneself in life means to cultivate a deep awareness of one's surroundings, emotions, and inner self, allowing for genuine connections and meaningful interactions. It is about living with intention, finding joy in the journey, and being open to the richness and diversity that life has to offer. Ultimately, immersing oneself in life is a continuous journey of self-discovery, connection, and embracing the magnificence of existence. It is about understanding and cherishing the incredible gift of my presence within you while exploring the wondrous depths of both the world around you and the life flourishing within.

Me: You said we get to choose how we experience life. But we are not all given the same opportunities at birth. How, then, can we choose the life we want to live?

God: True, not everyone begins life with the same opportunities or advantages, but the power of choice extends beyond one's initial circumstances. Your ability to shape your lives is not solely defined by the hand dealt at birth, but also by how one responds, adapts, and grows in the face of diverse experiences and challenges. Yes, everyone does not get the same parents, body, treatment, or material possessions.

However, the constant presence in every life is Me—I am always here with you. The diversity of experiences, the uniqueness of each individual's journey, and the varied circumstances encountered are what shape each person and the world in profound, precise, and distinctive ways. Choosing the life, we want to live does not always mean changing external situations, but often involves transforming our responses to them. It is about making the best use of the opportunities available, adapting, and finding ways to create new paths. Immerse yourself in life by seeking knowledge, learning new skills, building resilience, and making conscious decisions that align with your aspirations—then taking action. Consider one of the most powerful gifts that is bestowed upon you—imagination! It is high functioning in the beginning periods of life and for some it tapers off quickly.

Think back to when you were a kid and you could create new worlds and ways of being in your mind—the world, even the universe, is/was truly yours. However, over time, many influences alter one's thoughts, perspectives, and realities and the magic of imagination is diminished. So, keep the little kid in   you alive, always—continue to dream and work toward those dreams, use your imagination to help shape the world around you. The ability to choose how you respond, how you nurture your imagination, and how you pursue your dreams remains within your grasp. It is this unique amalgamation of experiences, choices, and resilience that defines the course of your life, guiding you towards fulfilment, growth, and the realization of your true potential. Dream it, will it, act on it.

Me: Sorry, but what does that even mean when You say, "I am always there." There to do what?

God: As I am, You, are! As I am, all things are! I am there in the background leading and guiding those who listen. This means you have more power than you think—this power is literally at your fingertips awaiting YOU!

Me: So, I hear what You are saying, and maybe it just hasn't sunk in yet, but what can be done to mitigate taking on someone else's perspectives and thoughts?

God: It is inevitable that you will acquire influencing belief systems, perspectives, and ways of thinking. These need not define you, however, view them as experiences to learn from, insights to reflect upon, and mirrors to better understand yourself. By cultivating self-awareness, practicing discernment, and grounding yourself in your own values, you can integrate what serves your growth while letting go of what does not. In this way, the perspectives of others become guides, not chains—shaping who you are becoming without eclipsing your own truth. One needs to be OPEN to EVERYTHING and ATTACHED to NOTHING (NO THING)! Be open to the possibilities in everything—as anything is possible—but remain detached or unmarried from all things. In between you will find Truth!

Me: People are always in search of purpose, what is our purpose?

God: (jolly laugh) The purpose of life is nothing more than to be purposeful, but it is a choice for each person to make. Be purposeful in the small things. Like making it your purpose to make someone smile or laugh, making it your purpose to check on someone during difficult times, making it your purpose to help or give back to others— just be purposeful in all you do. Through purpose comes passion, through passion comes gratification, through gratification comes fulfillment, through fulfillment comes liberation! Simple, yes!

Me: Why did you give us the power of choice?

God: (grinning) It is your birthright and one of the best gifts I could have given to you! Choice is an open expression to be individually and openly different, to be who you want and what you want to be under the limitations you (You) define for yourself. Be that which you were meant to be, create that which you want, Build! This gift will take you on the journey of a lifetime and will show you that there is so much beauty in this world! However, (stern look) be mindful of the illusions of the world!

Me: What illusions?

God: Anything you perceive as real!

Me: So, are You real?

God: If I am not real, who are you talking to right now then? (hearty laugh) I AM as real as "YOU" are. That which is real can never be destroyed or changed!

Me: That's a little misleading, isn't it? You just said I am as real as You, however what is real can never be destroyed. I'm a little confused? As far as I know, if the body dies, that means it is destroyed—how can I be real?

God: If all you think yourself to be is the body, then you will be just that—merely a body or a corpse!

Me: I guess I must spend some time on this...

God: Indeed!

Me: How do You feel about religion?

God: (light sigh) Religion is great at its core, and I have been there in the hearts and minds of man through every step of writing the great books. However, the minds and hearts of man have been infiltrated by what you call, Ego! Religion is great, but not necessary. What you all call spirituality is My essence! Religion is like fruit; it is just part of the tree—that is Me!

Me: With the many religions and belief systems of the world, what should we call You, or what is the proper way to address You?

God: Call Me no-thing! Address me with sincerity and love. Talk to Me as you would yourself or the true love of your life, and see Me in all things with no bias or limitations. No mortal name can quantify the entirety of what I Am. To come into My presence, learn to just Be— be still, be quiet, and be in the moment!

Me: What about those who hate or have biases and infuse those beliefs with a "higher power" through indoctrination or religion?

God: (look of great disappointment) As I have mentioned before, it is up to each individual how they choose to live. However, it is the duty of each person to elevate their consciousness and for those with elevated consciousness to help those without. This goes to what I said about openness and being unattached. Challenge the word of man and seek wisdom in Me or counsel in someone *truthfully* wiser than yourself!

Me: Respectfully, I feel there is hate in the world and there are many in "power" who use their positions and titles to push their agendas, what is to be done about this?

God: Yes, (sigh) hate disrupts the natural order of things, invoking chaos. This is never good, yet it is needed from time to time and takes much to rectify. Biases are natural and can be swayed. They should always be challenged within the Self—if not by yourself, then by others in a noninvasive manner! Those who use religion—or, more precisely, their own narrative version that they call religion—to motivate their self-interest and persuade the masses in under-handed dealings are a danger!

Me: So, what should be the main focus as humans, then?

God: Again, as I have mentioned before, you have the freedom of choice to focus your life on whatever it is you want! Just know that the only way to truly be free is through an absolute understanding of Self!

Me: What do you mean by *"truly free"*?

God: What keeps you wanting? Wanting more—more friends, more likes on your social media, plastic surgeries, clothes, new cars, jewelry, etc. But always feeling unfulfilled. Cash-in on Me or pay the price! (slight pause) The thing you all call as "spirit," is the essence of Me! So, as you are born into the physical world, most—but not all—assimilate and conform to the world around them. When this is done, an ego is formed. This ego can blind you or bind you. It can hinder you from being the greatest version of You (which is Me). It will make you feel inferior to most or all and create what you call, as Hell. Hell is a state that is created in the mind and manifests into the body or physical existence around oneself. This Hell comes in the form of negativity, doubt, stress, fear, disobedience, and dis-ease. Bring awareness to those things that do not cost and which truly matter in life, then you will truly be free.

Me: So, if at the core of each of us You exist, then why does so much bad—or what we call "bad"—happen?

God: If you absolutely knew that I existed in you, would you still act in indecent and un-Godly ways? One must dive into the Self to know thy Self. What you call "bad" things happening, happen to ensure that one understands and appreciates what "good" really is. As a neophyte (NEO) in this game of life, a dualistic response is used until life is seen as a whole and truly becomes (ONE). When the NEO is ready it becomes the ONE!

Me: So, how do we attain this freedom you talk of?

God: (subtle laugh) Through Me! However, one needs to explore, learn, and understand who one is at their very core! It takes the removal of distractions to place focus on one's Self! In doing this, you will find that you were and have always been free!

Me: I understand! But, what steps should we be taking? As, I have conformed to this physical world and have allowed myself to somewhat become corrupted, how do I get back to You?

God: First, know that I have never left you—I am with you always and will remain forever. Second, every soul is born into this world carrying baggage, woven into its memory This memory often imprints itself upon the body as fear, self-doubt, hatred, and other negative patterns. Such coding is cyclic in nature, repeating from generation to generation, until one becomes aware of it and finds the courage to break free.

Me: So, why does this happen?

God: (shaking head) This question "why" is very active in the minds and mouths of the youth. It is a question that seeks truth, understanding, and an innate quest for knowing. It challenges the status quo. As an adult, answering the question of "why" must be handled with much grace and the utmost of care. It is the duty of those in question to answer with truth or find one who can, so as not to continue the cycle of unknowing. Discussing the "why" of something challenges both parties— challenging one to speak with complete comprehension and the other to respond in such a way that is not "because I said so" or "that's just the way it is and has been." This requires all involved to think about their "Why" and answer in the most truthful and graceful of ways. Now to answer your question, this happens as a result of the complex interplay between human free will, societal influences, and the inherent struggles of existence in the physical realm. Over time, negative patterns and behaviors become ingrained within individuals and societies, perpetuating a cycle of suffering and disconnection from the divine. Breaking free from this cycle requires conscious awareness, self-reflection, and a willingness to transcend the limitations of the ego- self. It is through this process of awakening and aligning with the higher spiritual truth that one can begin to dissolve the layers of negativity and reconnect with the divine.

So, one must counter this altered code by re-programming one's thinking, peeling back the different layers until one reaches the core—the true Self. What must be understood is, that which one accumulates in this existence and considers themselves to be cannot be You (the real or true You). What seems real is just a perception or an illusion!

Me: Ok, I think I'm with you for the most part...until you said, "That which one accumulates in this existence and considers themselves to be cannot be You or real." Umm, yeah, what does that mean?!

God: So, in essence that which you call yourself cannot be You! Is that any clearer? (chuckle)

Me: That which you call yourself cannot be you. (in my head: What in the world?) I have nothing. Can you elaborate, please?

God: So, let it be said like this—what you call as yours cannot be You. What you call as yourself— or what you think of yourself—is just a collage of learned behaviors, thoughts, traits, and acts all composed within the 5 sensory systems which happen all within you! Yes! So, the you, that you think is you...is not You! YOU must distinguish between the illusion of everything. That is the difference between your experience of things being inside versus outside.

Me: Ok, so what You are saying is much of who we are is just a composition of all we have learned through our senses—how and what we think of ourselves is an illusion of the senses? I believe I am starting to understand, but I'm still having a problem totally comprehending.

God: Yes, you are on the right track! Let's begin to transcend the limits of your mind and surpass this so-called "perception" you speak of. Let's say, for instance, that you currently know there is life in you by touch/feeling, taste/eating, sight/seeing, hearing, and smelling, Yes! Now, suppose you could not touch, hear, smell, see, or taste. How would you be able to experience life right now?! When you fall asleep this happens to some extent—"you" do not experience the senses and essentially "you" do not really exist. There is no perception of physical reality as you know it, and there lies the illusion! One has seemed to have forgotten their true identity and one tends to identify with their thoughts and body. Now, if you are asked "Who are You," and you do not identify with anything whatsoever, who is it then "You" become or what or who will you find?

Me: My mind is...

Me: Let's change pace for a second. How are you doing today? What is or does today mean for you? Does time exist for You?

God: (chuckle) Time? Time is a simple construct. It can be used to track cycles as well as manipulate and theorize what you consider to be reality. As I am the beginning and ..., time is like a line, spiral or bubble that continuously goes on. You can think of it like a circle or bubble that is ever expanding with many infinite pieces, all with different interactions which create and tell their own stories. However, to answer your question, "today" in your terms is just happening with all of creation in the now. Time has no relevance to Me, but I am good—very Good. Let's just say I am perfect, always!

Me: God, why are there so many religions in our world? Is there a right or perfect one? What are we to learn from them all?

God: Learn everything that you can from them! There is good in all that is good as I *am* good! But be weary of alternative motivations and the influence of man...or the ego of man. It is easy for one to confuse the best intent I have for you versus the best intent *they* have for you! Question what does not seem "right" or "good." If you listen closely with a still mind and heart, you will always hear Me and know the truth!!

Me: What happened to the minds of man—and by man, I mean all people? Was man ever perfect?

God: Is not everything perfect? Man's body and mind are perfect! However, man's mind and body have become corrupted with man's illusion of self (ego). Yes, there is such a thing as a perfect form of man, however that which is perfect must absolutely know Me!

Me: What happens when we die?

God: Depends on how fast you want to find out! (hearty laugh) That is a question most humans are fascinated by, yet never get a chance to discuss. When one's last breath leaves the body, so does one's energy (source energy) or consciousness and spirit. It leaves the physical body and transports to a place that is neither here nor there, yet is everywhere and nowhere.

Me: What are we here to learn if death seems easier than life at times, especially since we're born to die?

God: Yes, death may appear to be an escape, but to wish for it is to miss the greater picture. From the moment one enters the physical world, death is already in pursuit. Though death is certain, let it serve not as an enemy, but as a quiet teacher—reminding us to cherish each step of life's journey. So live as you choose, yet remember—it is worthwhile to learn, to explore, and to experience all that life offers. Live with enjoyment and fulfillment—create action- filled and purposeful intent, for in doing so you draw closer to the Self that is Me.

Me: In today's society there is much anxiety, fear, and depression. This can lead one's mind to catapult into a dark place or even have thoughts about hurting oneself. How can one counteract these thoughts and negative characteristics?

God: That which is ingested by the body and mind can purify or corrupt the mind, so beware of what goes in. Whatever comes into the body or mind through the senses has an effect. It is important to recognize the profound impact of what we consume—both physically and mentally (food, TV shows, social media, music, air quality, self-talk, or the simple touch of another person). Our senses are constantly bombarded with stimuli, and each input leaves its imprint on our consciousness. Thus, maintaining a sense of balance and purity in our consumption becomes paramount. This includes not only the food we eat but also the media we consume, the air we breathe, and the interactions we have with others. Moreover, in navigating the complexities of modern life, it becomes essential to discern between reality and illusion. Much of our suffering stems from our attachment to perceptions and desires that are not grounded in truth.

Understanding that our true essence already embodies the qualities we seek—love, beauty, fulfillment—can be a powerful realization. The journey then becomes one of self-discovery and acceptance, recognizing the inherent divinity within oneself. The practical application of these insights lies in affirmations and intentional acts of self-love and appreciation. By consciously affirming our inherent worth and beauty, we begin to shift our perspective and cultivate a deeper sense of self-compassion. This process is further augmented by immersing ourselves in the beauty of nature, which serves as a tangible reminder of the inherent harmony and abundance present in the world. Ultimately, the path to overcoming negative thoughts and characteristics involves a holistic approach—one that encompasses both the puri cation of our external environment and the cultivation of inner harmony and self-awareness. Through this journey of self-discovery and self-love, we can transcend the illusions of suffering and embrace the boundless potential that resides within us.

Me: What is needed to be a better human?

God: The will to want to be better! As well as time in nature (grounding). Man has forgotten his relationship and bond with nature—when the two are out of sync, dis-ease and disease happen on either side. Meditation to cleanse and purify the mind and connect with spirit, balanced healthy eating, and light movement are all key for the well-being of the physical body. Again, an unbalanced lifestyle will cause dis-ease or disease and will quickly break down the Earth, body, and mind.

Me: In today's world there is so much diversity—which is a beautiful thing—however, there is also much division. What is needed to mend and overcome this downfall?

God: (a wondering grin) Yes, there is so much beauty in

diversity. And there is much diversity in your world, as well as in the universe. Everything works in unison and is in the most precise balance. One simple feat, whether macro or micro, can lead to the demise or extinction of a single organism, planet, or system. Now, understanding the ramifications of balance, what do you think happens with division? Things should be done with the mindset of the common good for all! So, pretty much do what's right all the time! So simple the hardest things become! (chuckle with a head shake)

Me: We all have this perfect dream of how we want to live—what stops us from living that dream?

God:(light chuckle) YOU, of course!

Me: Ok, yes, I believe that...but *how*?

God: First, remember those times as a child when you used your imagination to dream freely— dreaming of who you wanted to be, what you wanted to do, and even pretending you already had the things you longed for. In those moments, the universe was yours. Now, as an adult, you live within boundaries and limitations—some imposed by family, some by society, and some by yourself. These limits whisper what you can and cannot do. The key is that you must get your imagination back to those days of the innocent childhood and practice it with unwavering focus, over and over, until your vision feels alive within you.

Release yourself from the bondages and boundaries that have been placed upon you or that you have accepted as truth. Speak your desires into existence— breathing life into them by believing and feeling as though they are already here. This is more than mere wishful thinking; it is aligning your inner world with the reality you wish to create. When your words, emotions, and actions are in harmony, you begin to radiate the very energy of what you seek, drawing opportunities, people, and circumstances into your path. But remember: belief works both ways. Guard your focus, for giving life to the wrong thoughts can carry consequences that reach far beyond what you intend.

Me: Is there a right and wrong way to eat!

God: (hearty chuckle) Yes, of course—one should chew with their mouth closed so not to smack! Eating and not eating (fasting) with purpose is of the most importance. In today's world, many eat just to eat, or for convenience. One should eat for their lifestyle and respect all which they consume, as it was once all alive (or should have once been alive). Remember that at some moment it gave its life so that you might have continued life. Please understand that which you consume becomes a part of "you." If one lives a more sedentary life, eat mainly plants, veggies, and fruits—think of yourself as a grazing type animal.

Those who have a moderate activity level with daily light exercise should eat mainly veggies and fruits, and then add in some meat sources from the water. Those who engage in strenuous, laboring workouts or those who are athletic types are not limited to specific groupings of available food sources. But, remember, as in all things, balance is key. To assist the body with digestion and energy balance, it is best to eat heavier meals early in the day, meaning eating the heaviest proteins (animals) before evening. Then, have a light dinner of fruits and veggies to balance out the day. The choice is yours in how you eat—the outcome of what you eat is the result of much of the right things you put in your body compared to how much the body burns. All in all, enjoy different foods, but do not live for food or to simply eat food. Keep it simple—stay away from foods not made completely of nature, limit your alcohol intake (I would suggest absolutely none), and if you must think twice about eating or drinking something...do not! Simple, yes!

Me: You mentioned fasting...

God: Yes. Fasting decreases food consumption, which decreases strain on the digestive system. This lessened strain leads to an increase in one's overall awareness. Fasting expedites self-awareness in its many aspects of self, as well as increases one's connection with Me for those seeking.

God: Now, I have a question for you. How much is your life worth?

Me: (in my head, this is easy) There is no amount of money you can put on life, as it is priceless!

God: Why then do you not live as if your life is priceless? I give you all so many variables and unknowns in life with the hope that you will live it to the fullest. I give you all the latitude to live your best lives and do your best work but many of you have failed. You let the possibilities of "what if" or what will not happen overshadow the possibilities of what can—this is not of Me, as through me all things are possible. I am the I AM that can make all things happen! So, when you call on the power of, I Am, know that who You are calling on is Me! So, be careful in how you use I Am, for whatever you attach to it you will become. To think any other way Is a detriment to yourself and the world around you, just as fear without courage is un-Godly. Do not live a life just to die! LIVE in between the two extremes—live freely, lovingly, happily, and without measure! To feel and be stuck for a while is okay and happens from time to time, but understand that stagnation intertwined with complacency is an ultimate dismissal of Me.

Rhetorical Questions: Things to Think About

God: It seems as though you are always in search of perfection. Many change their appearance, change their thinking, and alter their character traits for the likeness of others, why? It pains Me to see something I have created perfectly be altered. Please know you are created perfectly for an exact purpose to be exposed at an exact time, *if* you choose to listen. I have created certain defaults (gifts) within you that keep you true and safe, it is a knowingness inside of you that will keep you out of harm's way! So, listen, and listen carefully.

God: (shaking "his" head) You all sure ask the question "Why?" a lot! (grinning) Why this, Why that? My question to you is, *why not*? In all the situations you have had to ask "Why," what did you learn, if anything? (stern look) I will wait, I have a lot of time! (hearty chuckle) In that time of need, heartache, disbelief, unknowing, and vulnerability, what did you find! Believe it or not, sometimes the "why" in certain situations is not for you to know and just is. There is no acceptance in the question "Why," and if there is no acceptance there can be no growth. If there is no clarity in knowing your "why," you have not learned your lesson or you have not completed your test/training at that time.

God: What makes one deny me for poor Earthly things? When you grow tired and weary of those things, then what? What then do you seek? More things! (hearty chuckle) Seek that which only one can find within the Self—that is unchanging and not of this material world!

God: If you take away all the physical aspects that you hold near and dear—like your sight, hearing, taste, touch, and smell—then take away food (as what you eat is the compositional makeup of the body), what do you have left? What is now your substance?

God: At the most basic level, to know Me you must first

come to know your Self. The same is true of love: to truly understand love, you must begin by loving yourself. Through self-love, you awaken to the depths of My love. Love can be learned—such as when you bring a child into the world—but the truest love is the love of Self. Be open to both giving and receiving love, like the sun to its rays.

Back to the Conversation:

Me: Why are we born into this world only to die in what seems to be a couple years in relation to planetary years? What is the true essence of this short time on earth?

God: Your time on Earth is relatively short, but what would you do with more? Better yet, what aren't you doing with your time now?! Every day is a day to be closer to Me, to help and uplift others—especially those who are lost—to live life to the fullest, and to be the greatest version of yourself that You can be! I have mentioned this before—the choice is yours in how you want to experience life. Go out and live a life truly worth living, because the only loss in life is when life dies inside you while you are alive! The short answer to this question is simply to learn and experience!

Me: If one's objective in life is the betterment of Self, how does one achieve this given the many setbacks in life.

God: Life is happening, whether you choose it or not. It happens to you, in you, through you, with you, and against you at times. In this, the choice in how one chooses to respond and handle life is of great importance. One's greatest setback will lead to one's greatest achievement—success and growth. Embrace and work through any setbacks or roadblocks as they help cultivate you into the greatest version you can be. On the other hand, it can also become one's greatest downfall. If the true aim of life is the betterment of Self, then the only real failure is giving up in the face of challenge—or never trying at all.

Me: What is "real" in the world?!

God: (sigh & grin) "Real" is that which one perceives by the senses in the physical world. However, where does everything happen—outside of you or within you? (subtle smile) Just as dreams happen and are experienced by humans, are they not perceived as real by the dreamers, at least in that moment? Where are dreams happening—to you or within you? Reality, as you experience it, is deeply personal and internal. It is worth contemplating: where do your experiences of reality come from? I know you seek answers, but sometimes the most profound truths lie in the questions themselves. When you look deeply enough, the answers are waiting before you—or better yet, within you. Real, as it relates to Me, is the unchanging state. What you call 'reality' is, for each person, an amalgamation of countless happenings. When these events are gathered in your awareness, they appear as a single thread of experience—something you may choose to call real through perception, or recognize more profoundly as truth through innate knowing.

Chapter 2: LIFTING THE VEIL THE JOURNEY WITHIN

Me: They say the truth will set you free, so why is that we must go around "Martha's barn yard" to find the truth? It doesn't seem that free. Why isn't it something that we just inherently know...is there even a way to just know? I guess I'm talking about universal truth, the truth of the ages, the truth of our earthly existence and beyond that is just unbeknownst to us.

God: Ah, the search for truth—a timeless endeavor that has perplexed and inspired humanity for ages. In many ways, the truth is everywhere, woven into the very fabric of existence, yet its discovery is often obscured by the complexities and distractions of earthly life. Yes, the truth will set you free. However, an absolute knowing is liberating. Nothing is without a cost! Just being an earthly inhabitant costs many things—time, joy, peace, health, wealth, and (at some point) life. If everything everyone wanted was just given to them freely, then what? If one attains millions of dollars over time, one learns how to respect, move, and use that money. On the other hand, if one gets millions of dollars suddenly without any knowledge or preparation of how to handle it, what do you think will happen to it? The truth is always there, waiting for your discovery.

What you seek is normally looking right back at you! You mention going around "Martha's barnyard" to find the truth, meaning the circuitous and sometimes indirect paths one takes in their search. These paths, though seemingly long and winding, are valuable in their own right. They offer lessons, insights, and experiences that enrich one's understanding and prepares one for the deeper truths that lie ahead. As for knowing the truth, yes, there is a way to "just know," but it often requires a shift in perception, a tuning into a higher consciousness or inner wisdom work. It is a realization that comes not just from intellectual understanding but also, from a profound inner knowing—a connection to the universal truth that resides within each being. Embrace the journey, cherish the lessons along the way, and trust that the truth is always there, waiting for your discovery. What you seek is normally looking right back at you!

Me: The fight is so, so hard! In trying to live and live righteously! But those who lie, cheat, steal, kill, and have an overzealous appetite, seem to get and have more than those who really try to do what's right! How does one make their heaven on Earth while doing the right things?

God: By doing the right things! (hearty chuckle) Along with doing the exact opposite of what you just spoke against! Yes, one's life might seem perfect on the outside, but what is going on inside? Are they healthy and joyous, do they know love, are they giving/sharing their abundance, do they truly know themselves? These are just a few of things that really count! Heaven in terms of

Earth is nothing more than a state of mind—you will definitely, not find it in the materialistic realm. One person will tell you life is hard and challenging, but another will tell you that it is great. The perspective comes from whose looking through the lens. As life is life, the fish, or the vegetables you eat might find it hard or unfair as they are caught or pulled from the sea or their roots and eaten. For you, my child, can flip any situation like a light switch—good or bad. Just like any perspective you accept, the concept of heaven or hell is first made in the mind. If you can have unrelenting focus, determination, and absolute mastery of the mind, you can control the outcome!

Me: I believe my greatest hindrance in this life deals with holding on to the materialistic world and at the same time wanting to be thoroughly immersed in spirituality. I tend to find myself at odds in wanting certain things, or the "finer" things in life, almost to the point where it feels as though I am cheating on my spiritual growth/attainment and feeling unworthy to have those things. Am I wrong to have these thoughts? Is it okay to want and to have these things and still attain spiritual enlightenment? Why does it feel so wrong at times?

God: It feels wrong because you have created two opposing sides. Just as a branch grows and splits in different directions, it is still the same branch of the same tree. Not being happy does no service to you! In your world and Mine, there is plenty. As you are already aware, material things come and go, as does the gratification received from those things. So, if it is the experience you are wanting, then experience it and enjoy it. However, be aware that where one places their focus, their energy also follows! Be present in life, as it is only happening in the now!

Concentrating on the many things that are not yet present will bring about much unease and suffering of the mind and body, which will compromise the spirit! The journey to Me has many paths, so be diligent in the pursuit of being the best version of You by experiencing all of Me. The spiritual path holds no value, for it cannot be measured; it is not a possession to be earned or gained, but a truth to be remembered. For the moment you turn inward, the eternal opens before you, and the journey both begins and ends.

Thoughts from Up Above

God: Through your experience, there is one Earth, one people (human beings with both feminine and masculine bodies, energies, and appearance), and many different species of organisms living together—no one is better than the other.

God: Land and the trees are plentiful, indeed, but are finite in magnitude. Please understand their purpose!

God: What is it that you take for granted? When you pause and reflect deeply, you may see that much of what you cling to is illusion—the very source of suffering and dis-ease. Consider this: life itself, at its most fundamental level, is what is most often overlooked. By this I mean the essentials that sustain you—food, air, and water. Look closely at what is happening to the very place you call home. At this fundamental level, there is a lack of respect and love for life itself.

This disregard has given rise to suffering and disease—seen in senseless violence, unchecked greed, widespread illness, and the countless struggles that engulf humanity. There are many philosophies and dogmas, none greater than another; all are paths meant to help awaken the Higher Self and move toward spiritual and personal liberation. But the journey begins here: love yourself first, and let that love flow outward into all that you are and all that you do.

God: Time with and within the Self are much needed by many. Take a moment to contemplate: How do you see yourself reflected in your own eyes, in the eyes of your community, and in the eyes of the world? Are you the giver of Self, generously sharing your essence and gifts with others, or are you the keeper of self, guarding and preserving your identity and integrity?

Consider your impact—how do your actions, words, and presence influence those around you and the world at large? Reflecting on these questions can provide profound insights into your identity and the legacy you are creating. This self-awareness is essential for personal growth, meaningful connections, and living a purposeful life.

Back to the Talk

Me: Whose path is it that I am following?

God: Depends on who you are following (lite chuckle). The deeper question is this: are you walking the path I set within you, or one handed down by others? To follow without awareness is to drift, but to walk with intention is to awaken. Know this—whether the road is smooth or rough, short, or long, easy, or hard, know that every path leads back to Me. What matters most is not the distance traveled, but the truth you uncover and the Self you remember along the way.

Me: It has been said life is an illusion. But if life is an illusion, how is that everyone can see the same reality (for the most part) with such differing perspectives?

God: Life is often called an illusion, not because it is unreal, but because it is impermanent and filtered through perception. Life is happening the way it is intended to—it encompasses the material world in which all are assimilated. All of life is happening at this specific time. However, it happens individually by all things at different levels as perceived by that thing. This is why many can gaze at the same cloud, yet each sees something different. The framework of reality is common—sky, ground, seasons, forms—but the mind interprets it in countless ways, shaped by memory, belief, and experience. This individuality of perception is the diversity of thought. To see beyond illusion is to look past appearances and recognize the essence beneath them. And this requires elevating awareness, turning inward to the source of perception itself. Begin by asking: Who is it that is aware of me thinking?

Me: As my intellectual mind tries to quantify what and who God is, what picture should come to mind that expresses You in the most perfect and subtle of ways that I can understand?

God: There are two distinctions. When one opens their eyes and looks in the mirror, what is the reflection one sees? As one looks into the mirror, one sees what they perceive as themself. Secondly, when one closes their eyes, what is it that one sees? The subtle backdrop of the eyelids creates a darkness, blackness, or nothingness. In between these two distinctions is how you should picture me. All that is seen is a reflection of you, which is the singularity of Me. Simultaneously, I am the possibility of all things, yet am quantified by no-thing. In short, I am everything and no-thing and all the spaces in between.

Me: What is the meaning of life?

God: The meaning of life is simple—to absolutely experience life through living life absolutely! Meaning comes *after* experience. Life is a simplistic test; however, the test is engrossed in an illusion that has been superimposed on itself, making it a masterpiece for the ages! The test is (game show pause) can you get back or simply remember?

Me: Help me understand this simple yet sophisticated, mysteriously majestic, hyperactive, peaceful, precise, artistically engineered play I get to star in! There are many stars intertwined in this magnificent thespian-like theatrical existence. And, depending on the optic beholder or sensory-tuned observer, reality seems to be a play on perception. So, when does one find the "real" in reality?

God: When one is ready—like the ultimate game of hide and seek—what is sought begins to reveal itself. The moment you truly seek, the path to discovery unfolds. The reality you live is but an illusion, shaped by shifting forms and fleeting experiences. What is real is that which never changes. To know the changeless is to know Me!

Me: I hear You, however I do not quite understand. You've spoken before about the illusionary world and how that which is unchanging is real stuff, but how can I get to a point of absolutely knowing the truth?

God: Some might say to do soul-searching. I say— explore the whole Self. This means exploring both the physical body and the unseen inner Self. Begin by bringing awareness to the body. Lie down or sit upright in a chair. Start with your feet: wiggle your toes, feel the muscles engage for a few moments, then grow still and simply notice the sensations—blood owing, nerves ring, energy moving. Slowly work your way upward— through the legs, the muscles, the joints, the organs, the chest, the arms, the hands, and finally to the crown of the head. Then bring awareness to your breath: inhale deeply and fully, allowing the diaphragm to expand, then exhale completely. Continue until your entire being is relaxed and in awareness. Now, let your eyes rest gently upward and hold the whole body in consciousness. Remain here as long as you can. This is the beginning of separating mind from body, the first step into your true Self. The power to do all things lies within you. The only question is—do you know it?

Me: Who God truly is, who we perceive God to be, and who we want or expect God to be are three entirely different things. How selfish it is for us to take what is unquantifiable, unlimited, and unimaginable, and attempt to reduce it to our own mortal needs—shaping the Infinite into a servant of our desires. Who do we think we are? Yes, God is all and can do all things, but what makes us believe that the Divine exists to answer our every beck and call? What causes us to look upon You in this way?

God: I am always here, happening in all ways—even in you. I am the smallest possibility of what can and cannot be. What makes one look at Me in this manner is one's bold imagination and uncontrolled ego. To do things in My name for the sake of one's worldly aspirations and selfish will is not Me. This will lead one and their legacies down a path of undesirable turmoil. In this experience, it is great to have and to be abundant, however true is the person who can have all things yet still put Me first as I am no-thing!

Me: Without a doubt, I see, feel, and in some measure understand the presence of a Creator—the universal Architect—especially when I zoom out and look beyond the routines of daily life. Yet I wonder: how can I truly experience that which cannot be seen, but is undeniably known? The more I seek to understand this Presence, the more it reveals itself, and yet the rabbit hole seems to get bigger and deeper at the same time. This existence feels like a masterpiece of abstract art: depending on the observer, the light, and the angle, the work can be interpreted in infinite ways. And so, I ask—what is it that You are truly trying to show me?

God: Only what you choose to see!

Me: That is very cryptic, yet profound! I guess that makes sense, as most of my life I have not truly known, what it is I want. If one's aim, vision, or goal is subpar or non-existent, one's journey becomes nomadic, incomplete, and unfulfilled!

God: Indeed, what is shown to you is an unmatched, unparalleled, theatrical performance that gives the beholder their own experience. For you, what should be noted is how You fit—to see from the micro to the macro, like an unlimited pixel being zoomed out. All things are of Me—your reflection is My reflection, how you see and treat others is how you treat yourself...which is how you treat Me! What can you be doing better? I challenge you to lead from your spirit and not from the body. You are a spirit having a physical experience not vice versa.

Me: I feel as though I hopelessly walk through life searching, working, and doing things. I do things that uplift my community, things that make other people happy (which is fulfilling), and I even do things that make me happy. However, those things only fulfill me for a brief moment in time. Then the cycle of trying to fill some void starts again—it's like a never-ending race! What is this feeling?

God: What is a void? At its surface, it feels like emptiness, but if you look deeper, it is never just absence—it conceals possibilities. This feeling arises because the things we pursue— achievements, recognition, even fleeting joys—can only satisfy for a moment, while the soul longs for something lasting. The void appears as a reminder that what you are truly seeking cannot be found outside of yourself. It is not a punishment but a signal, a call to pause, reflect, and turn inward toward the Self and the Source. Within this pause lies the chance to uncover hidden truths, to see what is waiting beneath the surface of your life. Rather than a hole to be filled, the void can be seen as a canvas—a place where meaning, growth, and self-discovery are painted through your willingness to engage with the unknown. To embrace the void is to embrace life itself, for it is in the empty spaces that your next chapter begins.

Me: Sometimes it's hard to pray or talk to a God I cannot see. How do I distinguish the voice in my head from You?

God: Which one is always right?

Me: Touche!

Me: Why God, why me?

God: Again, the question 'why' is always a hard question to wrap one's head around. An inquiry into 'why' often proves to be perplexing and challenging, an enigma that seems to resist straightforward comprehension. When this question arises from pain or struggle, know first that it is heard—that your experience is not ignored. In a curious way, it is a question that possesses the capacity to guide one along a circular trajectory, looping back upon oneself in an intricate dance of introspection. Instead of grappling with the elusive 'why,' consider redirecting the inquiry toward 'how' or 'what.' The 'why' might not always be a question meant for the one seeking answers; rather, it unveils itself as a profound consequence, intricately interwoven within the fabric of one's choices. The 'why' emerges as a direct outcome of the decisions made by an individual, sending ripples across the vast expansion of the universe. It is not a detached query but a reflection of the intricate dance between personal choices and the unfolding cosmos. Thus, the search for 'why' is less about receiving an immediate answer, and more about uncovering meaning through the living of the question itself. As one contemplates the 'why,' it becomes apparent that each choice, no matter how seemingly insignificant, resonates through the intricate web of existence, shaping the narrative of one's journey as well as the universe.

Me: What is life?

God: Anything at the most fundamental level which moves is alive! Life is a symphony of movement, a dance that unfolds at both the grand scale of the macroscopic to the intricate realm of the microscopic. It is a manifestation of perpetual motion— the beating, the pulsating, the rhythmic vibrations, and the ceaseless excitation. This knowledge will no doubt cause a fundamental shift in your core perception of life, transcending conventional definitions and delving into the dynamic nature of existence. Understanding life as the continuous motion at various scales prompts a reflective inquiry: What truly embodies the essence of life, and is it flourishing to its utmost potential? Merely existing, merely being alive, does not guarantee the infusion of life's vitality into ones being. Life, in its fullest expression, involves a harmonious interplay of purpose, passion, and fulfillment. Life is not just about being alive—it is about infusing every moment with action and passion that defines a life truly well-lived. Life, in its profound complexity, beckons one to move beyond mere existence and to embrace one's potential into something tangible, vibrant, pulsating, and rhythmic that propels them toward the fulfillment of their greatest capabilities. Life is the etheric thread binding all things—many forms, one essence.

Me: How do we unify the masses?

God: Depends on how great the cause! In today's time, people are so connected that they are disconnected! An unprecedented connectivity through technology, people often find themselves ironically isolated and distracted. While the internet and technology can be powerful tools for communication and knowledge-sharing, they can also be double-edged swords that pull people away from genuine human connection and self-reflection. To unify the masses, the answer lies within the question, specifically in the word unify. Much of what is taught especially from a young age causes division, causing a myopic importance of self which is heavily imbued in materialism. This indoctrination which is ingrained in greed and over-zealous need for power and control will continue to cause cyclical generation demise, which keeps you at a distance from ME.

If you are kept at a distance from Me, how can one unite and connect with those near and dear, much less those of no relation. True unity starts with making time for themselves, to reflect, to grow, and to serve others. Then through understanding, empathy, and shared purpose. Unification will be sparked by a common cause or shared values that resonate deeply within the people. By identifying and rallying around these shared principles, one can bridge divides, foster understanding, and create a sense of community and belonging that transcends geographical, cultural, and ideological boundaries. Yet even in unity, balance is essential—for anything taken to excess can become a chain. True connection must always serve freedom, not confinement, so that the You who is meant to be free can remain free.

Me: How does one find and truly become one with You in this existence?

God: Die! This is not a purely physical death, per se, but a death that releases one from themself and allows them to renounce all that one is attached to. To 'die' in the context of seeking oneness is not a physical demise but rather a profound transformation that liberates one from self-imposed limitations and attachments. This metamorphosis involves a deep detachment from all that one holds onto dearly. This journey towards wholeness requires a willingness to actively seek and entails a departure from the multitude of labels and identifiers that often define our existence— race, religion, economic status, emotions, fears, the physical body, and even the constructs of the mind. This metamorphosis involves a deep detachment from all that one holds onto dearly. It necessitates an acute awareness encompassing all layers of the self while simultaneously recognizing the awareness that transcends these layers. To truly find and unite with the essence of existence, it is imperative to traverse beyond the confines of societal constructs and personal identities.

It involves acknowledging the transient nature of these labels and delving into a deeper, more profound understanding of the Self. This journey toward oneness requires a conscious exploration, peeling away the layers of identity to ultimately realize the interconnectedness of all existence and the unity that lies beyond the boundaries of the self. Be aware of all levels of you (what makes up the self) and know the awareness that is.

Me: How real are you? How real am I?

God: How real am I? I am beyond what you call real—I am the essence of being itself, the unchanging presence in which all things arise and pass away. You cannot measure Me with the senses, for I am both within them and beyond them. And how real are you? We are as real as you allow Us to be. What is truly real goes beyond what you see, hear, or feel—into what you know, yet cannot intellectually explain. The body you wear, the thought you think, the roles you play—these come and go, but the essence looking through your eyes is the same essence as Mine. The longer one wrestles with what is real and what is not, the faster life passes by. For in truth, you and I are not two realities but one. I am as real as the love that breathes you into being, and you are as real as the awareness that knows this.

Me: How do we know what we're supposed to be doing, as life has many different hoops and hurdles?

God: One step at a time, one experience at a time. When you find yourself doing all the right things for all the right reasons all the time, then you will know!

Me: Is what we have in life ever enough? I ask because I know that I have all that I need, and I honestly feel as though I should want for nothing. However, I find myself mentally always wanting something more.

What is this craving I have?

God: (with a beaming smile) Ahhh, yes! Interesting that you use the word *craving*. This craving which you refer to is actually a seeking, an exploration, a searching, a longing, and a wanting to connect to that which makes you, You. You are merely trying to find that which is all encompassing and unchanging. This *craving* just needs to be directed and focused on, and in the right place (Hint: Within).

Mini Poem

A beautiful montage of the most exquisite colors serenading the canvas of life, this light like love which illuminates the backdrop of my eyes as if to say you've been touched by a presence which knows no bounds.

This movie projected through the eyes, which shines bright like the stars, who star in it. Just as the universe explodes and continuously expands, so does the soul of man want to expand in its physical existence, yet is caught in a tumultuous state and explodes in torment unknowingly because, unknowingly, He forgot.

In the depths of this forgotten truth, amidst the chaos and the noise. A glimmer of remembrance stirs, and a stillness beckons from within. A flicker of the divine flame gives birth to the infinite possibilities that await and essence of who we truly are!

In the subtle silence, I hear your whisper—magnificent and beautiful are your words, that blow passed my ears. However incidentally shrugged off like a suggestion, but hopefully it is captured by the mind's eye and delivered to heart to be acted upon with grace.

CHAPTER 3: THE PATH TO SELF-REALIZATION

Me: Who am I?

God: Many times, throughout life one asks, 'Who am I?' It can feel like an immense, overshadowing question, leaving many perplexed for the entirety of their lives. Yet the truth is simple when seen clearly—the answer lies within the question itself: I Am. 'I Am' is the essence of being, the awareness that remains before all labels, roles, and identities. As you contemplate the question, it is also important to turn your energy toward who you choose to become in every aspect of life. Then life and creation will have a funny way of letting you know who and what you are and have been!

Me: How does one create balance and fulfillment in every dimension of ones being, without sacrificing one for the other?

God: One must first establish a foundation of balance within the life forces—in the mind, peace; in the body wholeness; and in the spirit, harmony. This balance is cultivated through practices already spoken of—fasting, mindful nourishment, quiet time, self-reflection, and, above all, listening to the subtle guidance of the Higher Self.

Me: How can I show up in life and put all I have learned into practice in a way that lessens pain and suffering each day?

God: In life, one cannot run—much less hide from—pain and suffering. It is inevitable unless one can see pleasure and pain and joy and suffering as inseparable aspects of the same whole. Choose, then, to show up fully in life: be present, meet all things with clarity and courage, and hold your head high—as to know no difference between joy and pain.

Me: Hey God, is there a difference between dreaming, wanting, and desiring something? Is there wrong in any of these?

God: To dream brings wanting and to want brings desire! To dream is beautiful because it calls on the imagination and a childlike innocence. Think of dreams as the water source of an infinite ocean. Like waves or ripples, it holds all the endless possibilities of what can, what may, and what will not! To want is to bring about the subtle movement of dreams, like a quiet pond that has been disturbed by a pebble being dropped in it. It is a transfer of energy. The want of man is a build up from man's dreams, from something so big and abstract to something that begins to be more precise and have more focus. The dream is the initial energy that can move a want into action. Be careful, though, for a want can change direction and become monstrous like a tsunami wave. It can consume and control the mind, causing uneasiness as to make one depressed, angry, jealous, or sick! Be mindful of where you place and direct your focus, as energy flows where the mind goes; and it does not matter if it is good or bad.

Desire is the concise focusing of a want that sets a large amount of energy in motion to bring a dream into motion—from the abstract world to the physical world. It is like a magnet, attracting what one hones in on. The stronger the magnet, the stronger its attractive ability. So too, the stronger one's thoughts on a desired dream, the more one is able to manifest what is desired.

The desire must be strong enough to bring about a consistent persistence of action toward that desire. However, do not allow one's unfulfillment of the desires of their heart to cause the soul to be held in captivity or enslavement to that thing!

Me: Hey God, I'm having issues with what other people may think of me. How should I handle this?

God: Trying to think about what other people are thinking will cause a great deal of anxiety, stress, and suffering—there is already much going on in one's own mind. For starters, when you look in the mirror, what do you see and think of yourself? That is all that should matter! If negative thoughts arise, it shows much is still needed to be done in learning how to control the mind. Work on the areas of your life where lack and negative thoughts about self-arise. To think about what another may or may not think will lead to madness and unrest. Stop!

Quick Thoughts:
If God were to come back now, would you recognize Him? Would you deny Him? The answer is that most would

deny and pass God off as crazy. This is so because most do not recognize the Divine inside themselves!

It is funny you think of Me as this big guy in the sky—I am the You in your Self!

Time and space are ever expanding within the confines of an unlimited cloak—celestial bodies so enormous the physical mind could not fathom. In this, you think you're a big person!

Life is very precise at doing what it is supposed to do. Life happens as it is supposed to, however, how are you happening?

In asking for help in the things that are desired but not needed, one should ask for protection from the self that is not You.

Back to the Conversation:

Me: You seem to like stretching the limits and bounds of our physical, spiritual, and mental capacities! What are we to find from this?

God: Good question! After much dialogue between us, I hoped to have "sown" a piece of Me in you. What do you think the answer is?

Me: Well, from what I think I know, life seems to be a compilation of many tests. Each test expands our fundamental knowledge, but also gives us wisdom in each of the three aspects of self until there is no difference. I believe these limitations are another test to bring us closer to knowing that limits and bounds are just illusions. The more we understand this, the more capable we become. The more capable we become, the more we grow into the infinite nature of You and truly begin to know all things are possible!

God: When you begin to understand—rather when You know—who is in You, around You, and through You at all times, there is no reason to fear and nothing you cannot do!

God: What is that I owe you? Because you sure ask and whine about many things, especially when things do not go your way?

Me: I guess you're right...well I know you're right! Many of us act as though we are the sun and everything revolves around us in our self-centeredness. Yet, in all honesty, you have out done yourself with everything. Nothing is owed because you have provided everything for us and I believe it is up to us to experience life in its many diverse faculties in order to figure out what it is *we* owe *You* to some extent!

God: I see! As you would say, can you elaborate on what the certain extent might be?

Me: Yeah, so I believe we want to experience life the way we want, when we want all the time. However, I believe that in doing this we would miss out on so much. The profound paradox of experiencing life as we desire or envision carries with it the potential for missed opportunities and a diluted understanding of life's intricate lessons. Life unfolding exactly as we wish, without unexpected twists and turns, might inadvertently shield us from essential aspects of the human experience. Like pain, an inevitable companion on the journey of life, which serves as a catalyst for growth, a sculptor of resilience, and a testament to the array of emotions woven into our existence. However, without the bitter-sweet contrast of life's challenges, the fabric of life's experiences would lack the true meaning of joy. Without confronting the challenges and uncertainties that inherently accompany our human experience, the interplay of joy and sorrow, triumph, and setback. We will have missed out on the profound insights into understanding ourselves in the midst of getting back to You.

Me: The human body seems like the perfect "machine" for a lack of better word, how is it that humans come about getting so many ailments and diseases of the body?

God: Much of what happens to one's body is caused by them. It is caused by the way one eats, one's environment, how one thinks, and how one's spirit is aligned with the body. It is the true, cliché trifecta of mind, body, and spirit. Please understand what goes into your being will have a profound effect, whether that be positive, indifferent, or negative. Do not merely observe what enters your mind or body; instead, be diligent and attentive. Be compulsive to an extent in your awareness, and approach it with absolute mindfulness as you only get one physical body so cherish it well.

Me: I respectfully ask why is it that babies and kids get cancer or unwanted diseases at young ages?

God: One might see the physical world as imperfectly, perfect. Your perception of "bad" things happening in this existence is perfectly happening the way it is supposed to. In times of suffering and adversity, the strength and resilience of ones being are often tested and revealed. It is an invitation to deeper introspection, compassion, empathy, and the boundless capacity for love and kindness that resides within each soul. Each soul enters this world with a sacred purpose—one that transcends the limitations of time, age, and even physical experience. Though it may feel incomprehensible, especially when we witness the suffering of the innocent, such as babies or children afflicted with disease, their presence and path are not without meaning. These young souls, in their brief yet radiant journeys, often become profound catalysts for awakening in those around them—opening hearts, shifting perspectives, deepening love, and reminding us of the fragility and sanctity of life.

Their suffering is not a punishment, nor a reflection of divine absence, but rather a mysterious unfolding within the grand design of creation—shaped by mysteries one may not fully understand from their limited vantage point. Infinite wisdom and compassion, holds every soul gently, no matter how short their earthly stay. Even in pain, there can be unseen grace—a ripple of transformation that touches lives far beyond what the eye can see. Trust that every soul's journey, no matter how brief or challenging, contributes to the greater evolution and unfolding of the universe. Embrace the mystery and find solace in the interconnectedness and sacredness of all life.

Me: Who is the devil, may I ask?

God: Why? Is it someone you would want to know? (chuckle) Whether the devil is real or not is a matter for one to decide. In most cases it is man's ultimate adversary, the person who is reflected in the mirror when one is by themselves. Side note, why breathe life into something that is known to be inherently malicious and unpleasant?

Me: So, what is right and what is wrong, then?

God: One might think common sense would be enough, yet in this day and age it is often overlooked. Use the mind to analyze with clarity, allow the heart to feel, and guide, and when that is not enough, trust the instinct of the gut. But be cautious—the heart can be easily swayed, persuaded, and even blinded by emotional attachment, which can distort the senses and the other faculties of self. So, when faced with choices of right and wrong, good, and bad, let your final counsel rest with Me. Come to Me in stillness, meditate with Me, and you will know the way!

Me: What is the most insightful, breathtaking, inspiring, or captivating advice you can give me?

God: With every inch of life, you move an inch closer to death—at least in the physical sense. So how would you live if you had only a week? A day? An hour, or even a few minutes? What truly matters, and what does not? How have you impacted your family, your community, the world? How do you treat others? How do you see the person next to you? How do you see yourself? One should be full of life—overflowing with joy, never stagnant, ever expanding. Cultivate yourself and those around you. Love every facet and dimension of life, and seek with enthusiasm that which is seeking you: the unknown. The greatest gift I give to you is life in the physical. In life, and through life, so much—or so little— can be accomplished and experienced. Therefore, in life you are asked to live fully, and with life you are asked to give freely. Regardless of the path you choose, the potential of life is exponential!

Me: It is said that I am an unlimited being—how is it I do not know the capabilities of my true nature/potential? Better yet, how do I begin to tap into this next level of capabilities within my Self?

God: You are indeed unlimited, carrying within you all the potential and energy of the universe. Yet much of this boundless nature goes unrecognized because you identify with the limited—the body, the mind, and the stories you have been told. Layers of conditioning, fear, and distraction blind you to the vastness of who you are, just as clouds conceal the sun. The power has never left you—it has only been obscured. Still, potential alone is not enough. If you do not harness it—focusing it into motion, into something tangible—it will remain only potential.

Dreams and aspirations that could have been will wither unrealized, leaving only the shadow of 'if.' *What if this? What if that?* The way forward begins by turning inward—quieting the noise, practicing presence, and awakening to the Self beneath thought. From this clarity, you must join potential with action, and action with purpose. Absolute focus is essential, but so is aligning that focus with intention rooted in your Higher Self. For when potential, action, and purpose unite, the shadow of 'if' dissolves, and what remains is the reality you create!

God: In the beginning of our conversation, you mentioned the death of your mother. How did you get through that time?

Me: I became numb for a while, even leaning on the bottle (alcohol) more than I should have. However, I was able to become aware that I was drinking a bit more and stopped. I leaned on family and friends and stayed busy with helping others. The patience and love of my wife, who was my biggest advocate during this time as she dealt with the passing of her father years before, was a huge help. There was a lot of learning and soul searching, most of which started before her death and absolutely helped in the preparation of her death. I have never had a problem with death, as I know it is one of the most natural things in this life and the only thing I know to be absolutely true, we all must face. We all must die—it is the end of the life cycle from what I know. Through observing death, I have come to respect life much more, trying to see myself in all living things. I have learned that life is truly a process with many phases or levels, at these levels or phases there are wisdom deposits. I have collected essential data in times of tribulation and times of good fortune—in both cases, something vital was learned for either present happenings or experiences later down the road for myself or others.

Me: Relationships between married couples seem so hard to maintain, especially in today's society which is full of many distractions. How can couples have longevity and keep that so-called puppy love constantly going? How does one achieve an everlasting, loving, and harmonious relationship?

God: I would like to know what You think?

Me: (sigh) I'm not entirely sure what I have learned, but I will share my thoughts. To love and be loved is truly remarkable. To share your life with someone who sees the essence of who you are—even if only most of the time—is a gift. It is a joy to have someone to be affectionate with, to grow alongside, and to share the responsibilities of creating and nurturing life. Yet, as beautiful as that sounds, I know it doesn't always work so seamlessly. Sometimes, no matter the depth of love, it feels as though love itself isn't enough.

As two people grow, so too does their love—but not always in the same way. And perhaps it is meant to change, for everything changes. Love only needs to remain true to the spark that first ignited it. But what happens when love no longer feels sufficient? In my experience, a relationship becomes a mirror, reflecting not just the other person, but one's own inner conflicts. This is why self-exploration is crucial—peering deeply into the essence of one's own existence. Communication is paramount. It requires time, reflection, dedication, and even prayer—both alone and together. It also means cherishing the joys, both past and present, and finding happiness even in the midst of challenges. Love is not simply about what you feel—it is about what you choose, about what you create, and how you nurture each day.

God: This is well said, grounded in your introspection, and lived experience. A relationship at any level first happens because two people choose to be in that relationship. That relationship must be met with equal amounts of energy or strain, as pressure or stress will be introduced from either side. A relationship has many dynamics, can have many moving pieces, can feel overwhelming, can be easy or straight forward, and can be this or that. When the puppy-love phase passes, then what? What is the foundation of your relationship? Have you established goals, shared beliefs, and the small nuances that keep you connected? What do you want from your partnership? What must each of you learn to grow and change together—to share communion, to listen with intention and speak with grace, to choose each morning to love, respect, and trust?

The biggest takeaway is Self-knowledge and identity—an art too often lost today but returning. Spend time examining your thoughts and how you can be better; with steady practice, you will become better—and so will the relationship.

Me: God, who or what are You?

God: The very essence of creation, however, call Me no creator, yet I give the power to create. The cause, yet not the effect. The essence of perfection and beauty, yet not what makes something perfect or beautiful. The essence of nothingness, yet the embodiment of everything. The essence of Life, but can show no one thing how to live. The essence of all matter (seen and unseen), yet not what makes things matter. I am the incomprehensible essence of all things.

Me: What makes me unhealthy?

God: All things that do not serve one's complete Self will cause imbalance. Many things fall into this category—unbalanced eating, pollution (environmental, sociological economic, psychological), frequency disruptors (music, television, social media, fear, ego-driven people, and lies, to name a few), and even one's own thoughts. To be unhealthy, one need only believe themselves to be so. Yet awareness is the key. When one chooses to align with truth, nourishing both body and mind, balance returns. As the body reflects the mind, so too does the world reflect the collective state of thought. In health lies not only the power to heal, but the remembrance of the wholeness that has always been within.

Me: Hey God, how are we supposed to know You care for us? Because at times it seems You may not...?

God: Please expound!

Me: Well, it seems as though there is so much bad that happens in the world and when you zoom in to each individual there is a lot in one's own life that could be considered as bad that happens. However, when we call for You, it seems as though You are not there or are quiet!

God: Interesting! Everything you truly need is already provided. I give you all that is necessary, though circumstances may shift from time to time. Understand, my role is not to be your personal genie, granting every fleeting desire—so do not confuse passing wants with genuine needs. Learn to value what cannot be bought above what carries a price. For if I stepped in to remove every hardship or shield you from all adversity, how would you ever grow stronger, wiser, or better?

How would it help you draw closer to Me? More importantly, how would you discover what you are truly made of—or who you really are? How else would you come to know your own limitations? With much of what you call 'bad' that has happened, ask yourself: what was learned, what was gained through those experiences? Perspective and thought must shift if you are to move forward and grow. If so much 'bad' seems to surround you, then ask—what within yourself can you change? One thing is certain: I am always with you, and I will never abandon or mislead you. Keep speaking with the You that is Me—pray. Remember, just because things do not unfold the way you want does not mean they are not unfolding exactly as they should.

Mini Poem - Giving

The sun gives its all each day—every hour, every minute, every second—before it tires and passes the torch to its sister of the night. What it gives is unconditional, asking nothing in return, forever pouring itself out. It offers light and warmth that fuels life, restores life, and at times even takes life. Its perfect rhythm gives rise to a perfect relationship—a timeless celestial dance, entranced in the most enticing of spins, creating a union that has given its life to the giving of Life. To all the things we have come to know, to all we think we know, to all we cannot yet know, and to all we take for granted—out of this beautiful union, you have come: given life, given breath, given the earth to shape, to manipulate, to manifest as you will. Now that all has been given to you, the question remains: What is it that You choose to give the world?

Me: What am I?

God: That depends how one looks at the question. Without much elaboration, one could say they are a combination of atoms (spheres of energy and frequency), light and celestial elements precisely arranged to form the most perfect of organically operated mechanical bodies. All earthly bodies, no matter the species, in general get the same physical body whether male or female.

However, if one looks at the body as a vehicle with a specific make and model, the vehicle can come in different engine sizes, dimensions of size, colors (hue), and many other add-ons or modifications. The mind, or the vehicle's CPU, controls, and processes data from the senses—think of this as A.I. which is always learning and updating. If one looks analogously on the human body and the mind (CPU), hue-mans should see more likeness than what differs. Taking a step deeper—what You become or who You are when the mind and body are taken away are the questions one should ask! So, take time and ponder on this!

Me: How do we find who we are?

God: It all depends on where you look. (chuckle!) This is a question that requires much introspection and a dedicated focus. Spend more than just a bit of time contemplating this question with genuine intent in your heart and mind. Through this introspection, you will discover not only who you truly are but also your connection to Me. You have forgotten not only Me, but who You are, your own essence and origins. In a world filled with many distractions that consume the flesh, cloud the mind, and distance the spirit, it is easy to lose sight of your true self and your spiritual connection. Taking the time to reconnect with yourself and with Me will illuminate the path back to Your truth and self-discovery.

Me: How do I become more like You?

God: The interest in this question shows you are already on your way! Continue the pursuit of Self, investigating and understanding all aspects of you!

Me: I am so torn on how to live this life—or whatever this interaction is, this movie playing before my eyes. The struggle lies in choosing the right path: whether to devote myself to a spiritual life or to fully embrace the physical, living exactly as I wish. At times, the two seem divided by only a fine line; at other times, they feel one and the same. I am constantly being pulled between them.

As I search for clarity, I've observed that the senses are but illusions, casting clouds of confusion that obscure the truth. This makes it all the harder to know what is 'right,' or simply how to live. So, my question is this: how does one filter out all the unnecessary noise?

God: Choose Me...or, better yet, choose You over everything else!

Me: What does that even mean, choose You? I feel as though I am fairly in-tune with You and myself, but at other times I feel so out of touch with You. This might be a feat that only You can make happen! So, I DO—I choose You. What happens next?

God: Many times, in life, one prioritizes putting others first. Yet in doing so, the self begins to fade. To truly choose oneself, awareness must be turned inward— exploring the Self, communing with the Self, uplifting, and transcending the Self. Proclamation is only the beginning. Through devoted action and deep knowing, the truest reflection is revealed—a reflection that illuminates the narrow path back to Me.

Me: Hey God, what is it that You truly want? What is it that You desire from us? Or do You even 'want' anything at all?

God: To want is not in my nature, especially in your terms! What I like is to watch creation unfold under the governing planetary and universal laws and to experience what life is outside of Myself in you. As I am the heartbeat in all things—the subtle vibration seen and unseen, heard and unheard to those who choose to observe it—I want nothing other than continuous expansion in all things.

Me: What do you think are the biggest hurdle(s) humanity faces?

God: The greatest hurdle humanity faces is humanity itself—or rather, the lack of it. In truth, most things are simple. To be human is to have hue, or color; to be man is to walk upright with four appendages, bearing the genitals that produce sperm; and to be womb-man is to walk upright with four appendages, bearing both eggs and a womb. Yet beyond form, humanity carries a deeper responsibility: the responsibility to know oneself, to search, to question, to understand, and ultimately to recognize the You that is Absolute and Resolute. When this responsibility is neglected, humanity stumbles into division, fear, and forgetfulness of its true nature. But when it is embraced, the greatest hurdles dissolve, and what remains is the remembrance of our shared essence.

CHAPTER 4: REDISCOVERING YOUR DIVINE ESSENCE

Me: What keeps people stuck on stupid?

God: Within the construct of free will, each of you holds the power to choose where to direct your energy and thoughts. Yet those choices can lead to paths and outcomes that feel undesirable. To call something or someone 'stupid' is a less-than-extraordinary remark, for what appears unwise or repetitive is often the result of a complex interplay—emotions, past experiences, beliefs, and external influences all at work. Fear, in its many forms—fear of change, fear of the unknown—can hold one back, trapping them in patterns that feel familiar but are not beneficial. Added to this are societal pressures, low self-esteem, and a lack of self-awareness or reflection, all of which contribute to feeling 'stuck.' It is vital to meet this with empathy and support, remembering that every journey is unique. Be mindful of your actions and words, for even a single impure thought in the mind's eye holds the potential to topple an empire. Yet in the same way, a pure and intentional thought has the power to build one, to create life, and to restore balance.

Me: If we are "free," then what keeps us bound?

God: Attachment!

Me: Attachment to what?

God: SMH! (shake my head) My son, be mindful of anything that holds you back, that seeks to fill an inner void, or that offers only fleeting pleasure. Beware of relying on crutches or clinging to things not truly part of your essence, for they will only rob you of peace and hinder your growth.

True freedom comes from releasing attachment to external things and turning instead toward your authentic Self—anchored in truth, love, and the eternal. Attachment to any-THING is the chain that keeps you from Me.

Me: When can I have everything, I want?

God: When one is truly and absolutely ready, the question arises: what is one doing to attain what they want? If everything desired were given all at once, what else would one have to live for? One truly receives everything they want when they learn to desire no-thing. In releasing desire, fulfillment, is revealed as already present. In desiring nothing, you open yourself to everything—and life itself becomes the gift, presence.

Me: Hey God, in space there are stars and planets that make up what we call the universe. From what we or at least I can understand, this universe is ever expanding, ever moving, and cyclically trading energies. What is some information that You can share about space?

God: Space is nothing more than the passable area between at least two objects or things. (chuckle)

Me: No, no I understand that.

God: Just teasing! Everywhere and no-where, space is a fluidized media having no localized position however having an interconnectedness that is superimposed at every point and happening throughout the universe. Everything is connected through space, in space and by space. Space is the womb of all thing's material; it is the universal binding force that keeps everything together or in place yet is gentle enough where all things can move freely as they will. Space is the life force of the universe-like blood to the body, water to the ocean, air to the sky. Space in relationship to earth and humanity is a network or fabric medium that encapsulates and connects all things as it is formless. It is a media in which information, frequencies, energies, and capable beings can travel to capable recipients. Within you, space is the pause between breaths, the silence between thoughts, the stillness between heartbeats—reminders that what holds the universe also holds you.

Space is also an illusionary construct of the unseen, it is what unites the microcosm to the macrocosm where the imagined meets the precise, the precise meets the precious, and the precious meets perfection. At all levels all things exist here and interact in the most precise way- first under divine laws, then under the laws of interaction for each level of existence (existence can be quantified through levels of excitation low to high). The lower the energy or vibration of the creation the denser the creation, the higher the energy or vibration of the creation the more transparent the creation. Space is not only medium, but a mirror. It reveals all things by reflecting them, yet clings to none—an eternal witness, both holding and freeing all that appears. You are not merely in space;

you are space embodied—the same vastness condensed into form, experiencing itself. Space is not confined by time, but like a beautifully orchestrated melody it blends with the rhythmic heartbeat of all. Space is the gateway to the infinite and the doorway for the mind. It is the endless possibility of what is, existing as a momentary happening, yet expanding and changing as the mind changes with each new thought.

Me: Hey God, as you have created all things and created us in your image, what is it that you want to experience with us? What is the result of us being created?

God: The result of you specifically being created in the physical plane has yet to happen and is happening in the now. The path you are on now is helping you acquire all the necessary wisdom and knowledge to be used in the near future. The result of all things being created lies within the experience of each individual thing, as that thing and the resulting multitude of interactions between that thing. Each generation gives rise to the next, carrying forward the seeds that bring about the most precise changes—whether in the form of order or of chaos. And in the space between order and chaos rests the eternal question: can you remember who You are?

Me: How do we come to know Your true essence, when most of us hold only a conceptual or perceived notion of You—one that too often exists only to serve ourselves?

God: The truth is simple: the essence of Me is the essence of You, discovered only as you come to know yourself. Who and what you choose to serve is entirely up to you. Yet remember—what you choose to serve will, in turn, serve you in the way you allow it. So, choose with great care!

Me: Respectfully, You, seem to give answers yet not fully answer all questions in detail, why is this so?

God: The way you relate to the physical, the self, and Me is worked out in the mind and in awareness. I answer without exhausting every detail to invite the true seeker to think, to turn inward, and to discover. Some truths must be known by living, not by being told, and I leave space for your freedom, your timing, and your growth— because that is where understanding begins to awaken.

Me: What stops me from being the greatest version of me that I can be?

God: What stops you from being the greatest version of yourself is not a lack of potential, but the illusion of separation from the Divine. Simply put, it is often a lack of knowledge, ignorance, or the comfort of staying where growth feels hard. Yet even these are not flaws, but part of the soul's unfolding— guiding you to remember what you already are. Fear and resistance are sacred invitations, not barriers. They arise not to stop you, but to strengthen you, acting as mirrors that reveal where the soul is ready to expand. The journey is not about becoming someone else, but awakening to the truth that the greatest version of you is already within—waiting to be chosen and released.

Me: Many people have hope and faith, which can lead one to believe that You certainly exist. How does one get to know that You actually, exist?

God: To have blind hope or faith in the unknown is brave and commendable; yet the truth of the unknown remains just that—unknown. True knowing and understanding comes only through experience. To know that I exist, you must first know that You exist—beyond the masks of role and identity, beyond the fears that cloud you, beyond the restless stream of thoughts, and into the awareness beneath them all. You come to know Me not through external signs alone, but through inner awakening. I reveal Myself in your stillness, in your surrender, in the love that moves through your being, and in those moments when truth stirs; something eternal awakens within you. Faith opens the door, but presence, humility, and trust allow you to feel Me. I am not separate from you—I am the space and light within you remembering itself. And when you truly come to know yourself, you will realize: you have never been apart from Me.

Me: It is said that reality is a perception and perception is reality! Which is real or the truth?

God: Depends on the lens doing the observing and how the mind interprets what it sees. However, there is only one truth!

Me: So, what we call "truth," is that real?

God: What you call "truth" often mirrors your current perception, shaped by experience, belief, and consciousness. But Real Truth—eternal, unshakable, divine truth cannot be grasped by thought or language alone. It reveals itself as you come into deeper contact with your own essence. You are still unsure if I am real, and you do not even know who you are, so you have no authority to talk about what is real—at least not just yet. First, find out if you are real, or where Your realness begins. When you begin to uncover the truth of who you are—not your name, your history, or your mind, but the still presence beneath it all, you will come closer to Me. For I am not a belief to be proven. I am the Truth that remains when all else falls away.

God: In a generalized sense, both scenarios can be real and true to an individual. From the perspective of the observer, perception can falsely lead to misrepresentation of that person or thing—it is better to know! Perception is an illusionary state and becomes real when one chooses to believe in something unknown. To keep it fundamentally simple, reality is made aware by senses and then perceived by the mind. As all things happen within one's mind, the illusionary state of reality becomes real when one chooses to believe everything is happening outside of one's self. So, in truth, much of what one lives is an illusion. Through all the mumbo jumbo, can you get back, get back to the source? Can you see yourself and your neighbor, can you see yourself and a speck of dust, can you see yourself and the largest star in the universe, can see yourself and all things as one and the same? Here you stand, as I Am!

Me: So, what happens if you have two people on opposite sides of a so-called "truth" one in total belief and the other in total disbelief? How should this situation be handled?

God: As I have said before, one should be open—yet unattached—to the possibilities of what is and the possibilities of what could be. Experience in any situation is the best; however, experience can come at opposite sides of the dilemma. Embracing diverse possibilities without rigid attachment allows for a broader understanding. Engaging in discussions rooted in logical reasoning and presenting factual evidence can help bridge the gap between contrasting beliefs. However, it is vital to approach these conversations with empathy, respect, and a willingness to listen openly without dismissing opposing views outright. It is through such interactions that individuals can strive for a deeper comprehension of differing viewpoints, fostering a more harmonious exchange of ideas.

Me: It seems the more I ask for, the more the opposite happens. The more I ask for happiness and joy, the more it's a fight to be happy and joyful. The more I ask for wisdom, knowledge, and understanding, the more problems I seem to have to work through. The more I ask for more money, the more that seems to quickly dissipate. What am I doing wrong?

God: Yes, things happen in the course of one's day or life that can alter one's joy or happiness, however the light switch of one's joy, happiness, peace, love, and emotions can be controlled at will. It is always best to be in charge of one's emotions, rather than one's emotions being in charge of you. Until one is absolutely ready to Be— meaning no judgment on either extreme and finding delight in all things—the fight for whatever it is one seeks will be just that, a fight! But understand this: in the pursuit of happiness through adversity, every trial is preparation. What feels hard is only the turbulence of the spiritual mind meeting the physical. Things might seem hard, but this is so due to the evolutionary updating of your internal operating software. Change is one of life's absolutes, and outdated ways cannot carry you forward. The things you seek are also seeking you, but you must be sure they are truly what you desire—and take action toward them. Desire without action leaves the door closed; action opens the way. When your foundation is strong—your knowingness of Self—your path to Me narrows and becomes clear. All roads lead to Me, and with Me there is nothing you cannot endure, achieve, or overcome.

So, learn to smile and be thankful in all things. Those things which you seek is already seeking you: sometimes it comes instantly, sometimes gradually, sometimes only when most needed—and always according to how you can receive it. Now I ask you—how are you receiving Me?

Me: In man's un-resting drive to decipher ancient texts and decode the mysteries of the past, one text in particular said, " So, God created man in his own image, in the image of God he created him." I hear this and look at this verse in much awe and wonder whether this verse is to be taken literally or figuratively. If one were to take this literally, would this mean You created your "Self" in the physical form as a human?

God: Both literal and figurative truths are hidden within these words. When it is said that man was created in My image, it does not mean I am bound to flesh and bone. Rather, it speaks of My essence within you—the spark of awareness, the breath of life, the power of creation, and the freedom of choice. The body is but a vessel in physical form, crafted as a reflection for the experience of this world. My image is not the body but the being, the awareness behind the mask. So yes, I Am within man, but I Am not limited to man. I remain the boundless Source from which your likeness flows.

Me: The computer/phone has made many great strides since its inception and continues to improve and evolve. They are great for many applications, as they help to somewhat improve our quality of life and level of amusement. However, what are they doing to our mental and overall, wellbeing?

God: You tell Me...

Me: OooK! Computers/phones have been great from a scientific perspective, and in general they help with staying connected with family, friends, and information near and far. They have been instrumental in solving some of the toughest mathematical problems, they assist in the mitigation of different issues, streamline certain processes, and help efficiently run businesses. However, computers have become a major crutch in most communities around the globe. They have lowered the utilization of the mind's ability to think deeply and replaced it with A.I., Google searches and swipes up/down or left/right. People use the computer to do much of their thinking—frivolous time is wasted surfing and scanning for amusement, truth is distorted, and social media has absolutely altered the perspectives of what was once thought of as fact. Computers have created less than stable emotional states, as well as an induced an atmosphere of laziness which is at an all-time high, to say the least.

God: Technology, like anything else in life, can be either your greatest asset or your greatest adversary—it all depends on how it is used. Whenever the creation begins to act as the creator, it becomes the responsibility of the creator to cultivate a healthy environment in which that creation can grow, serve, and evolve into its highest potential. Think of a well-tended garden: when cared for with patience and attention, it yields an abundant harvest. So, is with all things—whether a person, a community, or technology itself. The difference lies in attention and intention. If we neglect what we create, it grows wild and consumes us. But if we steward it wisely, technology becomes not our master, but a tool that magnifies what is best in us.

Me: What is man's obsession with war, violence, and killing?

God: It is an egocentric nature lead by man's self-serving desires of fulfillment to pridefully win or beat someone by any means, at any cost, at the demise of that person, tribe, people, or nation. This inclination often stems from a profound lack of respect— not only for others but also for one's own self. It reflects an inherent unawareness of one's own identity, a deficiency in self- understanding that perpetuates a cycle of generational inhibition.

The minds of individuals, under the influence of this cycle, remain untrained and inadequately equipped to engage in critical thinking. This deficiency not only hampers the ability to empathize with others but also contributes to a distorted sense of superiority, further fueling the pursuit of dominance. A failure to cultivate self-awareness, empathy, and a holistic understanding of one's place within the interworking of humanity leads to a disconnectedness of source within.

Me: What makes one abuse their body?

God: This happens as most do not know their body fully, much less their mind. This lack of knowing leaves the mind susceptible to being infiltrated by impure and negative thoughts, talks, advice, emotions, and energies. As this happens most are always running and creating distance from the Self. The greater the distance, the less one becomes able to function and operate with control.

God: Question, you say you believe, right? However, what is it that you are believing in?

Me: You, of course!

God: Are you believing in the hopes that I exist or do you hope your faith is not in vain?

Me: Honestly, that is a great question…but I am not sure I know the answer! I guess this is what I am seeking to find out, as I have dabbled in reading some of the so-called "great books" and religious philosophies. I feel like a guy who is extremely thirsty—who's cup is trying to be filled—yet upon being filled the cup keeps getting tipped over. The thirst is never quenched. So, what I have read and come to so-call experience seems just superficial, as I believe it has caused me to intellectualize You without being fully immersed in You. So, it is like I know *of* You, but do not *know you*. How can one have a fully immersive experience of You—one that is instantly or unmistakably known within?

God: Yes, yes, I understand. Any book—no matter how great—will never equate to the totality of Me. A piece of Me, yes, all of what you experience in your life are also just many pieces of Me. So, the way to Me is quite simple! Completely love yourself, then see Yourself, feel Yourself, and know that You are all things and all things are no different from you!

Me: So, what is the exact nature of this conversation? Who is that I've been talking to?

God: My child this conversation is no different than the millions of conversations You have had before. When You have talked with Yourself. When You have asked Yourself questions. When You have found solutions to problems. When You have given freely with no regard for nothing in return. When You have smiled and No one sees, yet the world can feel your joy. When You have loved in such a way life slows down and a mirrored reflection of Self is seen. When You have understood life is being created by You and happening to You at the same time. When You have realized fear and negative thoughts do not serve You. When You have learned to challenge any belief system. When You can just stop and find peace at any moment. When You can be detached yet be present in all things. When one can have a multitude of experiences yet can sit in one place, one will know the true nature of who they talk to or with!

Me: In what way do I know me or my Self?

God: That seems to be a question you should be answering. So, what do you think?

Me: I'm still learning. I know I am more than the body because I can observe it, influence it, and direct it, especially when I focus my attention. The mind feels like an entire world of its own. It seems to be the central processing center where memories are stored, and where thoughts, emotions, inputs, and responses arise. Yet, I also feel I am something beyond the mind—or perhaps beyond the brain—because I can observe that too. So perhaps I am the Self, the one who is aware of both the body and the mind, or something that transcends and gently guides them both?

God: Good, good! But how do you know what you call as, me or yourself?

Me: I want to say through my reflection in a mirror, or through how I feel. However, I know whatever I am aware of cannot be the true Self. So, if this is true, I've kind of lightly come to a place of nothingness. In this place of nothingness, I cannot quite see past or through anything, so I am unsure.

God: You are close and on the right path. Continue down this path diving deeper!

Me: In today's society there seems to be much suffering. This suffering happens in many forms and dynamics and affects each individual in different ways. What is the point of suffering, what is one to gain from it?

God: First, in understanding what you call suffering, one must know the root of suffering. One constant in life that all must acknowledge is death (meaning all life comes to an end in the physical sense). In between life and death, there is change. Because of death, one is born into suffering—everything in the physical world decays and at some point, dies. Decay causes aging and the breakdown of all things in the material world. This aging and breakdown are where suffering is found. The point of suffering is important in decision-making, vital in knowing life, critical for growth, and essential for perseverance. Yet suffering is not only for endurance—it is also for awakening. In suffering, the illusions of permanence are stripped away, and what remains is the remembrance of the Self beyond decay. It is through suffering that one is invited to return to the Divine within, to see that what dies is not who You truly are!

Me: When I sleep, where do I go? If I did not wake from a sleep, where would I go?

God: Sleep is a lite detachment from the perceived self—certain meditative states and physical death lead to complete physical detachment. Where one goes during this detached state depends on the soul's readiness;

where it desires to go, where it is need to go, and what it is called to experience or remember. This liminal or excited state becomes a sacred crossroads where the seen blends with the unseen, where unknown meets the known, where flesh meets spirit, where self meets divine, and where everything becomes a simple play on itself.

Me: Where do we find You?

God: I have done much answering, so how about You tell Me!

Me: Well, I would think I would find You everywhere and in everything!

God: Yes, yes! But what have you learned from our talk so far? Go deeper to truly know!

Me: Ok, You are in everyone and everything. So, if we use our earthly senses to take in everything observable to us—meaning when we use our senses, they all happen from within us. So, you are always happening within us, right?!

God: Yes, so when you come to innately know this without the use of the earthly senses, you will come to know the being within and just be!

Me: Who is it that is aware that I am thinking?

God: When one becomes aware of their thinking, one transcends what is consciously and subconsciously known to be thought and one separates from the body/mind, thus becoming a part of a higher conscious mind that is mine! In between the removal of body and mind there you shall find the You, you are searching for!

Me: It is said we should see You in all things and all people. How are we to do that when some things seem inherently ugly or when it's hard to see the good in one, as their actions show otherwise?

God: Just as you may see something or someone as ugly, that very thing or person may see you the same. Yet as I Am, all is a manifestation of Me—from the vastness of the cosmos to the smallest particle, from the visible to the unseen. What you call beautiful or ugly are only shifting perceptions, reflections filtered through limited senses. I am the essence at the core of all things—beyond judgment, beyond division. To see Me in all, you need not excuse harmful actions, but you can learn to separate the essence from the behavior. By practicing compassion, patience, and humility, you begin to look beyond the surface into the deeper truth: even those who act in ignorance still carry the spark of Me. When you honor this truth, what you see begins to appear whole, purposeful, even perfect. For what seems ugly often reveals your own shadows, and in seeing through them, you remember: every face, every form, every moment is but a glimmer of the Divine unfolding through the mystery of life.

Me: What makes it so easy for many to not to believe in the existence of a higher power or in the existence of God?

God: Oh, yes, yes! One of the most fundamental and persistent challenges is that humans have tried to humanize Me—shaping Me through the lens of their own limits in an effort to grasp what transcends form. In their attachment to the personal self, they attempt to define the Infinite. But between learning and knowing lies a sacred space: the state of unknowing. This realm unsettles the mind, which craves certainty and tangible proof—wanting to grasp what is real through sensory validation. And in times of uncertainty, it becomes easy to disbelieve in what one has no understanding, connection, or experience. Yet as I have said before, one of the greatest gifts given to you is choice. You may choose disbelief, or you may choose to seek and to open yourself beyond the limits of the mind. Choose freely— but choose wisely!

Me: Who or what is ruling or controlling me?

God: The '*who*' is you, of course! However, what truly controls you depends on which version of 'you' is at the helm of your ship. The aspects of yourself you most identify with govern the natural programming of the mind. These influences come in the form of concepts, theories, stories, dogmas, religions, falsehoods, and controlled knowledge. Over time, these constructs evolve into belief systems that pull the strings of your actions, rather than your actions being guided by the One—the unchanging, eternal You.

Me: What is meant by unchanging?

God: Come, come! That which changes is easily swayed, moved, or flip- flops like day to night. Like a leaf in the wind, like one emotion to the another. Life as to death— that which changes cannot be eternal. That which is unchanged is and will always be!

Me: I feel as though You have created the grandest game of hide and seek or the most elaborate play ever. What I mean is that You have made each one of us unaware of our true nature, unaware of our true essence, and unaware of our truth that is You. What's more, we interact and act according to this unawareness. We are playing inside this grand play that is always keeping us seeking, seeking to find that which is You! Why is this so?

God: If all was known, how would the experience or experiment of life be? One thinks the experience of life is just for you? Big man on a small planet, are you? (Chuckle) I veil Myself not to hide from you, but so that you may awaken to Me by choice, not compulsion. What is freely discovered is far greater than what is forced. Unawareness gives you the space to act, to choose, to feel, to wonder—and in that wondering, to remember. Without seeking there is no discovery; without the journey, no realization.

Me: As individualized pieces of the One, what makes humans detach from You?

God: As individualized pieces of the One, humans detach from Me due to distractions, ego, desires, and the allure of materialism, which can cloud one's awareness creating barriers to My divine connection. This is an insightful question that one should reflect upon throughout their lives. While there may be clutter and obstacles to navigate before finding the 'yellow brick road,' challenges and disturbances can still arise even once your path is clear. How will you respond? How will you listen, act, and ultimately arrive at your destination?

Which path will you choose? One cannot truly detach from that which is inherently a part of You. However, one can choose to turn away from My light, creating a distance from Me that results in a sense of darkness. In this absence of light, individuals may inadvertently find themselves stepping into the realm of shadows. Here, the harmonious symphony of existence becomes disrupted, and the delicate interplay of life transforms into a quarrelsome interaction, reflecting the choice of the operator.

Me: How does one gain ultimate mastery over self?

God: Stretch!

Me: You got to be kidding, right?

God: No!

Me: How can stretching help me gain mastery over myself?

God: The body is a complex and intricate system, comprising various parts, functions, processes, and happenings all working together in harmony. What you instruct the body to do; it does within the limitations you have placed on it. Stretching initiates a deeper, more intimate, and in-depth connection with the body. Stretching serves as a bridge that opens communication channels between the body and the mind and the mind to body, at the most fundamental level. It allows you to become more attuned to the subtle sensations, movements, and capabilities of your physical self. It is worth noting that the physical body is generally the most accessible and straightforward aspect of our being to influence and manipulate, followed by the mind, and then the spirit. Utilizing stretching as a tool for self-discovery and mastery enables you to gain insights into your body's strengths, limitations, and unique characteristics. Initially, stretching may feel uncomfortable or even painful, especially if your body is not accustomed to the specific positions or angular postures involved.

Ease into each stretch and maintain it for an extended period, it is essential to tap into the calming and grounding nature of the breath. Focusing on the rhythmic flow of your breath will help relax your muscles, increase flexibility, and enhance overall well-being as you embark on this journey of self-exploration and bodily mastery. In time, this practice becomes more than physical—it becomes a doorway an awakening to the vast potential that lies within you.

Me: Thank you for always being there with me and for me!

God: It is funny how you still think we are separate!

Me: What makes us hurt the ones we love most, the most?

God: Hurting those we love the most stems from a variety of complex reasons. In some cases, it is unintentional, a result of misunderstandings, miscommunication, or even personal issues that cloud one's judgment or behavior. Other times, it is due to unresolved conflicts, pent-up emotions, unmet needs within the relationship and taking our loved ones for granted. Other factors like insecurity, jealousy, or unresolved trauma plays a role as well, to name a few. The aforementioned factors can lead to careless behavior or neglect, which inadvertently hurts those closest to one, often because one is projecting their own issues onto them. So, as one is still learning and mastering the self, one is still vulnerable to making unwise-choices. This can lead to paths of great disappointment and disapproval, which then causes hurt. In this, one still has yet to master the true essence of love. In the true essence of love, pain will never be deliberately inflicted upon a loved one if love is always place first!

Me: How did I come to exist as the "I" I am familiar with?

God: The "I" which is described is nothing more than the ultimate actor, the most prolific actor to exist. The "I" is the simplest form of You or a localized singularity of source experiencing dimensional aspects of reality in the physical form. "I" as a letter holds much simplicity, however as a word it becomes one of the single most complex words in existence. The "I" you speak of is not merely a product of circumstance or chance. It is the culmination of countless experiences, thoughts, and interactions woven together into the fabric of your being. From the moment of your inception, you began to shape and define this identity, influenced by the world around you and the choices you have made along the way.

The "I" is both the observer and the observed, the thinker and the thought a mini reflection of the divine spark within each individual. It is the essence of consciousness itself narrated by perception and ego.

To truly understand the nature of "I", one must delve beyond the superficial level of identity and ego, into the depths of self-awareness and spiritual knowingness. In this journey of introspection and discovery, the true essence of "I" is revealed not as a separate entity, but as an integral part of the interconnected network of one's existence.

Me: So, as many are in search for their individual purpose, what is the ultimate goal of this reality or existence?

God: As mentioned before, there is no need to search for purpose. Just be purposeful in your thoughts, actions, and all you do. However, find passion in something worth living for and apply action. Live up to the creative nature within you and help mold and create the outside world around you. Now, the ultimate goal in your existence is the true realization of the Divine within. This realization is an absolute knowing, the end of all suffering, and the be

all of absolute joy and bliss.

Me: What is it I do not know, yet that I need to know?

God: You don't know! (hearty chuckle!) There is much one does not know in their life and they will never know until they know! What you need to know is that when one needs to know they will find it when ready! What is needed to know is to seek and ask with clear and concise intention, then listen for the answer in the subtleness of your mind, heart, and being!

Me: So, God, as we have been conversing for some time now, I'm just going to straight up ask— what is the point of the illusions of self-versus Self, or the you versus You?

God: Yes, yes! It is now understood that there are two you(s). One is the body, carrying its roles, its reactions, and the shifting masks of identity. The other is the spiritual body, the True Self. Like oil and water, these two often appear to conflict when not in harmony. The physical body, being denser, often believes it is in charge, attaching itself to the many roles played in this life. And then comes the infamous trickster: the mind. In the mind, perception becomes reality—but that 'reality' is not always truth, for all is subject to change. One identifies as a race, gender, class, political belief, job title, parent, or citizen, etc. But these markers are mere fragments—microscopic reflections of who You truly are.

The illusion lies in believing these fragments are the whole. This illusion then becomes the lens through which reality is shaped and which life is lived. Now, to the deeper question: what is the point of it all? As I Am, all is. Imagine Me as the vast ocean and You— the Self—as a single raindrop. I Am the whole. You are part of Me, experiencing a fragment of the Infinite through a uniquely finite form. Life in the physical is a sacred test: you versus You. The man in the mirror versus the Awareness watching. This is the greatest play ever written, with each soul as the central character. The plot? A journey inward. A homecoming. The question is— can you find your way back?

Me: What makes people have anxiety from a young age into adulthood?

God: In today's world, there are many causes of anxiety, with factors such as inadequate preparation for life, pressure, an overzealous imagination, and trauma playing significant roles. Trauma manifests in various forms, whether through direct physical experiences or inherited genetic predispositions, where negative traits, fears, and past traumas are passed down to offspring. Trauma is also a learned behavior acquired through environmental and sensory input. An overzealous imagination grants the mind the power to conjure fears and negative scenarios, often leading one to anticipate and worry about events that may never come to pass. The tendency to catastrophize and envision worst-case scenarios can exacerbate feelings of anxiety and distress. Pressure can be a potent catalyst for anxiety, as the relentless demand to meet expectations, whether self-imposed or external, creates a pervasive sense of stress and apprehension. The constant scrutiny to perform at a certain level or achieve specific goals can instill a fear of failure or inadequacy, fueling anxious thoughts and behaviors. Preparation for life starts in the early stages of life and it is the duty of every parent—and their relevant community— to pass down the inherent and simplistic knowledge of common-sense skills.

Herein, lies the conundrum—as technology increases, life skills, and mental capacity decrease. It is important to know how to problem solve at every stage or level in one's life, as they enable one to navigate challenges and mitigate the consequences of ignorance or unpreparedness. Ignorance in and of the breath is a great hindrance in the evolutionary resolve of one to handle life simply within itself. As breath gives life to the body it accordingly conducts the symphony of life forces. Knowledge of breathing methods to combat any negative adversary of the mind is essential in fostering emotional resilience and combating anxiety.

Me: It appears everything in life is a test. What makes this seem so?

God: It keeps you on your toes! (chuckle!) For those embarking on a path of betterment of self, how would one become better without a challenge? How does one gain wisdom without first experiencing tests? Test and heartache seem hard, however look at what one has gained and what can be achieved through adversity, which creates newfound knowledge and wisdom. Adversity is the cultivator of experience, experience is the cultivator of knowledge, knowledge is the cultivator of action, action is the cultivator of life, life is the intertwined cultivator of spirit, and spirit is the doorway to the Divine!

Me: What is the true underlying cause of suffering—whether it appears as unhappiness, pain, illness, anxiety, depression, disharmony, deterioration, or frustration?

God: The underlying cause of all the forementioned struggles, is life itself. Rooted in the complexities of existence and material attachment. From the very moment of birth, life introduces pain—beginning with the labor of the mother. Yet within this first crucible of pain blooms one of life's deepest connections, a bond born of love and joy. To comprehend this existence, it is vital to discern whether it is the mind, the body, or the being that governs. The harmony of these faculties—when aligned and working together—determines the welfare of the greater self.

Ignorance of this alignment blinds one to the power already within. Thus, it becomes imperative to recognize and cultivate awareness of the being within the body, by the body, through the body— so that the being may govern with clarity and authority over all faculties of self. For in this alignment, suffering reveals its deeper purpose: not merely as pain, but as a guide that awakens us to the strength, love, and wholeness that have always been present.

Me: Many people throughout the world pray. It is a way of life for some, used as a way to meditate, used for placing blessings upon self and others, and used in the times of crisis or only in case of emergency. What does prayer actually do? What effects does it have? Is there a right or suggested way to pray?

God: Prayer is power! It is the subtle ability to use the influence of that which is unseen upon that which is seen, in a way that (if willed correctly) can have the utmost of positive effects, no effect, or something worse than what is prayed for. Prayer is the highest and purest form of thought.

When done right, it is the moment one intertwines with the Nothingness. In this purity, in this darkened polarization of the mind, the vibration of light transmutes prayers (thoughts) into something tangible, depending on the intent it is backed by. What you think of as prayer (communion with God) is just powerful self-talk. So, be careful what your thoughts are focused upon, as focused thought precipitates a focused outcome. Intent backed by the heart and infused with the will of the spirit creates and builds one's true reality.

Me: Coming from a perspective in which one's culture, roots, and heritage were lost due to life's turmoil (meaning not knowing where one physically comes from due to forced migration) how does one find who they are?

God: Knowing where one is physically from, as well as understanding one's family tree, helps shape the overarching self. It creates a sense of pride and attachment to one's environment and family, grounding a person within their culture. To know one's tree of life sheds light on ancestral stories, which in turn reveal traits, characteristics, personas, features, and even royal roots of past creators and past lives. Not knowing where you physically come from can itself be an illusion; for to truly know yourself—and to understand where you come from in contrast to the Divine—is the key to awakening from illusion into truth. As one opens to Source energy, perception begins to shift to a higher knowing. In this state, perception gives way to truth, and in that truth the question of where one physically comes from becomes irrelevant.

CHAPTER 5: THE ULTIMATE ACTOR UNVEILING THE 'I' BEHIND THE MASK

Me: How does one achieve what they want in this life?

God: To know what they want of course! Life is setup for one to be successful, to be the greatest version of themselves they can be. But please know you are already great! Now, in knowing this there are many obstacles, distractions, and matters of self that can lead to the sabotage of your greatness. What is truly needed in this life is to first achieve a knowledge of self. This knowledge of self is the greatest treasure in one's life, which leads to one's greatest success.

Me: What is the self/Self?

God: The self is a mixing pot, a collage of all of what makes you, You! The self has many aspects and layers. The self is a composition of what one might see as me or the reflection one sees when looking in the mirror. The self is also the unseen aspect of the inner happenings of the mind and body—the energy and life forces within and around. The self as the body is one of the most complex and masterfully built organisms on this planet. It enables one to mechanically take on everything from feats of great magnitude to the most simplistic feats of nature. The self as the mind is dynamically, intellectually, impulsively, and emotionally ever-changing and egotistically busy.

The mind is more than just a brain, more than just random and focused thoughts, more than a trans-receiver of earthly information, more than a storehouse of emotions, more than an autopilot system that seamlessly governs the body, and more than a processing unit to imaginatively and cleverly navigate the many aspects of the earthly realm. The mind is the bridge that connects all that is unlimited (understand the word unlimited) to all that is physical. The Self as the spirit is absolute truth, an absolute knowing, and a complete expression of freedom and expansion! It is universal—all things have access to it, as all things are it.

Me: After hearing this, is the spirit dormant within us? What makes it so hard to hear from the spirit?

God: Density!

Me: DENSITY!? What do You mean Density?

God: Yes—density. The physical body is like a lead weight in water: the weight sinks because it is denser than the water. The mind, however, is like a leaf; it can float upon the surface, yet with the right nudge or condition, it too can sink. One is embedded in the physical—embodied in a body, interacting with life through a multitude of senses. This immersion shapes one's perspective and experience, drawing the awareness deeply into physical reality. In turn, this creates distance between spirit and one's recognition of it, as the physical becomes mistaken for the true Self.

Because existence in the body is so saturated with the sensory and material, one identifies with this reality as their totality. It becomes heavy, intrusively tethering the self to the physical and making it difficult for spirit to guide and protect. Yet when one is ready, and releases themselves from the grasp of the lesser self, they discover that to be submerged in the water is not drowning, but immersion in spirit—the very essence surrounding all things. What once seemed dense becomes light.

Me: How does one reach or realize the full potential of what it means to be human? What does it even *mean* to be human?

God: Potential has many degrees, ranging from negligible to as vast as the mind and body will allow. To realize one's potential, one must first know one's limits— and then summon the will and action to transform possibility into something tangible, even kinetic. To be human is to be what you are right now: a body with its faculties, a mind with its processor and shifting states of consciousness, organs that distinguish life's generative design, and an essence charged with the current of universal energy. Few reach the fullness of their potential in this lifetime, and many only glimpse it too late. Yet to be human, at its core, is to live fully, to experience wholly, and to touch the vastness hidden within the ordinary. Simple, is it not!?

Me: Why should one have faith?

God: To the one who struggles with faith, I invite you to pause and look at your life so far. Where do you feel there is something missing? Where do you feel weak or uncertain? Ask yourself honestly: how strong has your faith been? What have you let influence you, distract you, or cloud your vision—keeping you from the strength and peace within? Having faith is honorable. But to walk in true knowing is to walk in alignment with truth—and that is where real power begins. You ask why one should have faith. Because faith is the bridge between what you cannot yet see and what I have already placed within you. Faith is the seed of your awakening; it activates your divine inheritance long before your mind can comprehend it. Even when your eyes fail you, your soul remembers. I have never left you, not for a moment. Faith is your lifeline to that remembrance.

Me: What does it mean to live or be alive?

God: What a beautiful question! You take a shot at it!

Me: To be alive is not the same as to live—though the word 'live' resides in 'alive,' the meaning can be vastly different. One can be alive and yet merely exist, drifting through time, observing life as it passes. This state is survival, not soulfulness. To live, however, is to be enthusiastically engaged with life—to be absolutely present in the now. To live is to know the cat and mouse game of life, death is always giving chase to life. In this knowledge, what has one come to know? What is one's ledger? And what is the edge of one's ability? What one comes to know is based on tangible experience or deep remembrance. The ledger is what one has done to this point in life— what is one's impact on/in life and what was not done that should have been done? One's edge means how hard and how far one can push—what is one's limit or one's will? To live is to explore yourself— the world, the cosmos, and the vast universe within—as well as the world around you. It is to seek understanding, over-standing, and inner-standing of the connection between the One and the whole. Through this immersion in life, and by living your absolute truth, real expansion begins. That is when life no longer happens to you, but through you.

God: There is one truth. Know who you are and live forever. Well said!

Me: I know we kind of touched on this, however for more clarification, who is the "I" and who is the self?

God: At this point in our conversation, you should be able to answer all questions from here forward. It is of absolute importance to first believe in and trust You—the Self. You are now connected, tapped into that which IS. It is equally vital to keep the body and mind clean and at optimal performance: fast often, declutter, and detox, so that a transmutable resonance of information may downlink with the Self and be used freely for the betterment of the All. The 'I' can be seen as the individual, or as the many pieces that make up the individual—it is the great identifier. It may appear as the mind, the body, or whatever it associates itself with. The self is the combination of all these 'I's—the ordered building blocks of the body and the inner components of the mind. This aspect of 'I' may be considered the self with a small s. The Self with a capital S is the universal, dimensionless state of You—the eternal 'EYE,' the UNIVERSAL OBSERVER. The Self is the absolute transceiver, relaying universal truth to the self, which ignorantly believes it stands at the center of the universe. Depending on one's depth of inner preparation, the 'I' can be seen either as the limited identifier—or as the ONE within the ALL.

Things to Think About/Food for Thought:

As you embark on this journey of self-discovery and growth, remember that each step forward, no matter how small, contributes to your evolution and to the betterment of the world around you. Embrace challenges and setbacks as opportunities for learning and refinement. Cultivate resilience, courage, and compassion as you navigate the complexities of life. And always remember—you are not alone. Seek support and guidance from those who uplift and inspire you, and in turn, be a beacon of light for others as you illuminate your path toward fulfillment and purpose.

The thoughts, statements, and questions that follow aim to awaken a deeper awareness of the true Self and to challenge familiar beliefs, ensuring you never grow complacent in your pursuit of growth. It is your responsibility to continuously strengthen the mind, body, spirit, community, and Earth—a commitment that must be woven into the fabric of your being and honored as an ongoing process. These fruits of wisdom should be taken in thoughtfully, digested deeply, and acted upon with care, fostering a more profound understanding of both yourself and the world.

The power already lies within you, but it must be both believed and commanded. Trust that the Divine spark within you is never absent—it waits patiently for your recognition. When you align belief with action, you call forth the infinite potential that has always been yours. And in living from this place of alignment, you not only transform yourself, but you help awaken the same light in others.

- In the journey of unlocking the next evolutionary levels of awareness in the pursuit of Self, it is vital to discern between the illusory aspects perceived in what one sees (the seen or the object) and how one sees (the seer or subject). Let us embark on this exploration by starting with the eyes (Level 1), where we bring our awareness to this faculty. The eyes thus awakened transform into the seer, the subject through which perception occurs. For instance, consider a simple cup as the seen, the object that comes into focus through the eyes. Moving to Level 2, we delve deeper into the nature of perception. What lies beyond the physicality of vision? It is the mind. At this stage, the mind assumes the role of the subject or seer, while the eyes transition into the object. Here, the mind becomes the canvas on which the senses, emotions, and ego are painted. It is the mind that interprets and processes the information received through the senses, shaping our experience of reality. Continuing our journey to Level 3, it takes one into the realms of profound awareness. At this stage, we awaken to the workings of the mind, embracing its intricate functions—the senses that perceive, the mechanisms that process, the emotions that arise, and the patterns of the ego that shape our experience. Here, the mind itself becomes the object, and awareness emerges as the subject—the true seer. From here, one may continue to traverse the depths of consciousness, plumbing the vastness of the Self. Yet it is crucial to first master these three levels, for they set the foundation for all further exploration. They reveal the subtle interplay between seer and seen, subject and object. Through this path of self-discovery, diligently honing our awareness, we unlock the hidden potential within. With each level traversed, we peel back the layers of illusion and step closer to our true nature. In doing so, we transcend the boundaries that con ne us and move toward self-realization. May this journey of awareness lead one into higher consciousness, where the seer and the seen merge, and the unity of existence is revealed.

- In life, and because of life, there is death. Two sides of the same coin, these dualities have much to teach— love and hate, health and sickness, peace and suffering, joy, and sorrow, to name a few. Within one's lifetime, much can be seen, done, and accumulated, and a great deal of our experiences and outcomes—perhaps 70% to 90%—are shaped by our own choices and actions. Do not become lost in the small percentage, the 10% to 30% that does not go your way. For if you dwell on it, that small fraction can grow to dominate your life, turning into 70% to 90% of your suffering and disease.

- In the pursuit of purpose, you should ask yourself two questions. What is it that you believe in most? What is it that you want most? If they do not align, rethink what it is you truly want and believe in.

- What is it that makes you do the things you do?

- In becoming what one is meant to be, one realizes they have always been what they were seeking. Yet action is required to move from thought into form, from potential into the tangible.

- What is it that you think you know, perceive to know and what you actually know?

- As life begins with the breath, return to it in every moment—breathing deeply to remain balanced and relaxed, accepting life as it comes. The possibilities of life, and how you shape it, are endless; all is potential. Envision the possibility you desire as already unfolding.

- The boundless and formless part of you is always in pursuit of its true beginning, as Source or the True Self stay, out of its way or pay the price.

- Are you the self or are you the ego? Who or what is controlling you? What is the You and what is the ego; do you know the difference? What is the true nature of your existence?

- If You are not the body nor the mind, and neither the body or mind is You, who are you or what do you become?

- The choice in being Pleasant or Unpleasant will dictate the outcome of one's life. If one chooses to hold joy for the things one loves to do, one must walk in joy for the things one dislikes, as to know no difference between the two. Willingly or unwillingly, pleasantly, or unpleasantly, the choice is yours in how you want to experience life.

- There are many dynamics and interactions in this thing called life, how we choose to live in life is predicated on how well one governs they're life in the mental, physical, and spiritual aspects in the pursuit of Higher Self.

- We all have two you(s)—a small (you) which is totally reactionary lead by ego and a big (You) that is the true Self that is ever expanding and ever knowing. In short, it is our own unknowingness that keeps us in limbo until we dissolve ourselves of the small you to become what which we already were meant to be!

- Adjust and balance the mind, or life will seem to work against you through its misalignment. As the universe unfolds, the body responds in harmony—otherwise, it could not exist at all. When the mind falls out of alignment, it resists these natural processes, creating struggle instead of f l o w.

- As there are a multitude of thoughts happening in the mind, which thought becomes more important than the thought of God?

- Through the nature of one's thoughts, emotions, and actions, all of one's experiences are caused by them. How are you choosing to happen, as the experience is absolutely your choice!

- To be in true peace and bliss, free from bondage and suffering, one must lay in absolute awareness, free of the mind and body!

- If one's body is in an unpleasant state—meaning there is some type of dis-ease, pain, or suffering—would one be happy or sad? If one's mind outside of physical pain of the head or brain is in an unpleasant state—meaning anxious, sad, or upset—are these states happy or joyful? As one has ultimate control over the mind, one's path forward should be in choosing a pleasant state of mind, as anything other than that does not serve them!

- Much of one's suffering comes from not being present in life. Meaning seeing life as it is, not living in the past (what has happened, happened), and not living in the future (what has not happened, is being imagined). Living in these two realms—past or future—will bring about much unease as the past cannot be changed and the future has not happened. If one believes in a higher power and things are not happening one's way, ask this, "Whose reality am I living in?"

- Who is it that is looking through the lens of my eyes? Who is it that is aware of me thinking?

- One needs not seek additional adversaries, if one brings about stress or strain either in the body or the mind. One will slowly work against their self, not only in physical health but in many different aspects of life itself! Do not direct your own life energies or mental energies against yourself, as the very source of creation resides within one. If the source within begins to work against you, then nothing in this world is going or can save you!

The Absolute and The Realization

Absolute: There is only one moment—the present, the now!

Realization: Each day deserves more intention and awareness.

Absolute: Death is certain!

Realization: I am the master of my fate-do not let life pass you by!

Absolute: I have no control of when I die!

Realization: I have much control over how I live!

- The words that follow I AM also follow you! Be careful of what you think and say about yourself!

- One does not know who they are because they are not aware of who they are! Awareness of the Self is the bridge between illusion and truth.

- As one gazes into the unknown of space, seeking and searching for life outside of themselves, ask what is in space that is not already in You?

- What beauty technology is and has become, in its innocence and complexity. It makes one's life easier, allowing more time for whatever one seeks. However, with more freedom to do, the more time is wasted on distractions. With extra time find time to find Yourself!

- We asked for greatness from the powers above, but what we fail to realize is greatness is already happening within.

We were already made great, we just need to work to be the greatest version of ourselves or become the greatest version of ourselves, we are meant to be.

- As you come to know who you are, the true nature of what you are and why you are the way you are comes true.

- How big your problems are—what have You done before you come to God? It takes a lot of energy to be someone to many, but it takes no energy to be yourself!

- If one has no knowledge or perception of the reality one is born into, where would this unknowingness lead one?

- The more attention one puts on being the person, the harder it becomes to be the Self. Two kings cannot sit on the same throne!

- Have the ability to tap into the knowing while in the unknown!

- The most important aspect of life is the breath. Without the breath there would simply be no continued life. If life is controlled through and by the breath, imagine the other aspects of life that can be influenced by the breath. Learn to breathe properly, consciously, purposefully, and gratefully and the world will be Yours!

- Be kind, honor, and respect nature's abundance around you as it gives all unconditionally.

- Walk gently on this earth in balance, in beauty, and in honor of all things and everyone neighboring you.

- See no difference between yourself or others—everyone and everything is equal as life is life. Be respectful, kind, and find honor in all!

- Love in a way in which there is only one way to love. Be the love you want, even if it has never been given to you. In return, love in its abundance will come to you and be all you know!

- What if you saw God in the mirror everyday yet chose to deny Him?

- Inquiry into self leads to an acknowledgement of self. Acknowledgment of self leads to discovery of self. Discovery of self leads to knowledge of self. Knowledge of self leads to mastery of self.

- Mastery of self leads to liberation!

- If you are of divine spirit, live to your divine nature.

- Your life spark, your very energy, is powered by a universal and unlimited force. So, how are you working to your potential?

- As you come to know who You are, the true nature of what You are and why You are becomes true!

- We are born into this world with the understanding that we are someday going to die. So, it can be safe to say that we are born to die. However, before you die, have you found something worth dying for?

- To know the Self is to know success!

- One is already perfect the way they are, one just has to tap into their perfection!

- When learning something new or worthwhile, one must spend time on that subject in order to learn whatever that craft might be. How much time have you spent on learning or knowing yourself?

- If a person lives in constant doubt and negativity, they create for themselves a form of Hell. When they open to love, joy, and goodness, they taste a form of Heaven. Since all things are experienced from within, the choice is yours in how you want to experience life.

- How does the unchanging mind that sees through the eyes perceive the world as it interacts with the eyes?

- Have you completed what you were supposed to do in this life yet?

- Imagine being an eagle that is no longer able to soar, how would that eagle feel? Imagine being a human so full of life, yet not living life!

- We are an amalgamation of God—uniquely fused and intertwined by matter (the body) and spirit (the soul). These two energies often lie at the root of our suffering and unease. Born into this physical world, we grow attached to it, identifying with the body and with material things in search of a pseudo-joy. Yet what is bound to change can never bring lasting peace or true joy, for these are found only within. The tension between the spiritual Self and the physical self must be balanced if we wish to know absolute joy and liberation in this life. Neither should overshadow the other; they must dwell together in wholeness. This balance is achieved through discipline— discipline of the mouth, of the body, and of stillness. Discipline of the mouth means watching both what goes in and what comes out— not allowing the mind to act blindly with words that wound or sow resentment. Discipline of the body means tending to it with care, so it may serve rather than enslave you. And discipline through stillness meaning meditation, the practice that unites all facets of one's inner cosmos with the soul. In stillness, the path opens to freedom, divine connection, and the answering of intentions and prayers.

- What does not serve you, should not serve you...so do not let it serve you!

- As You stand face-to-face with the universe, what is reflected in the eyes of the universe?

Mini Poem:

Cyclic Death comes to those who think death is never near. Liberation cannot be found!

Fulfillment comes to those who know death is always near and live life wholly in its fullness. Liberation is near!

Eternal life comes for those who are aware that they are aware. Liberation has already happened!

Final Reflections: The Call to Discover the Divine Within

These closing thoughts aim to awaken a deeper awareness of one's true Self and challenge even the most established beliefs, ensuring we never become complacent in the sacred pursuit of self-discovery and growth. This calling is both personal and universal: a responsibility to elevate mind, body, spirit, community, and Earth. It must be ingrained at the very core of your being and embraced as a lifelong journey.

Every step forward—no matter how small—contributes to your evolution and to the betterment of the world around you. Embrace life's challenges and setbacks as opportunities for learning and refinement. Cultivate resilience, courage, and compassion as you walk through the complexities of existence. And always remember: you are not alone. Seek guidance from those who uplift and inspire, and be a beacon of light for others as you move toward fulfillment and purpose.

The pearls of wisdom shared here are not to be rushed; they are to be taken in thoughtfully, digested deeply, and acted upon with care. For the power to transform lies already within you—but it must be believed, and then commanded.

At the heart of this journey is a truth revealed again and again: to truly understand the Divine, you must first embrace and nurture the divine essence within yourself. Through introspection, meditation, and the courageous act of living fully, you discover that the path to awakening is not paved by external validation or worldly pursuits, but by an unshakable connection to your inner Self.

Trusting the process of life becomes your guiding principle, reminding you that every experience—whether joyous or difficult—serves a higher purpose in the great tapestry of existence. Every decision, no matter how small, shapes the trajectory of your destiny. Through conscious choice and deliberate intention, you guide your life toward alignment with your highest purpose. Imagination, once feared or misunderstood, is revealed as a sacred tool of creation. When harnessed with awareness, it dissolves limitations and births infinite possibilities.

Amidst the illusions of the material world, truth becomes clear: love and authenticity are the ultimate realities. Through unconditional self-love and compassion, you awaken to the inherent beauty and divinity within yourself and all beings. The breath—often overlooked in its simplicity—becomes your anchor. Each conscious breath draws in the vital energy of existence, a living rhythm that connects you directly to Source. In its steady flow lies the gateway to peace, clarity, and higher realms of awareness.

On the path of self-discovery, give yourself grace—deep, gentle grace. Awakening takes time, and like a flower, the soul does not bloom all at once. Every setback, every pause, every breakthrough is part of your sacred becoming. At the center of this becoming is self-love. To love yourself is not selfish—it is sacred. It is the foundation that keeps you whole, teaches you boundaries, and reminds you not to seek worth outside of yourself. In loving yourself, you rediscover the truth: the Divine is not distant or hidden. The Divine lives within you, as you.

Self-love becomes the bridge between the seen and the unseen, the doorway from seeking to knowing, from separation to unity. In loving yourself fully and unapologetically, you not only transform your own life—you awaken to the truth that all things are connected, and that you have always been part of something infinite.

And so, this work, *Discovering the Divine Within: A Text Message with God,* invites you into a lifelong dialogue with the Source of all. It reminds you that the quest for truth does not begin outside, but in listening to the quiet whispers of your own heart. It is a call to remember that you are already a reflection of the Divine.

The final truth is simple: *To find God costs nothing— yet it requires practice. Practice as if God is always with you. Practice as if the presence of God surrounds you, moves through you, and lives within you. Breathe deeply. Live fully. And above all—discover the Divine within You!*

What makes the mind so noisy or active with its many thoughts? How much of what you think about is truly worth the time spent thinking about it? Is there a God? If so, where is the location of God? Who or what is this voice in my head? What am I? Who am I? If a tool is created for a specific task or purpose, are humans also **DISCOVERING THE DIVINE** created for a specific task or purpose? How many realities exist, as reality seems to change from person to person and mind to mind? If there is only one reality, what prevents us from seeing it as it is rather than how we think it should be? The mind is vast in its many interactions and dealings—what gives it so much power that it can also be fragile enough to deceive? Why **WITHIN** is it so difficult to see the Self? Why is exploring the cosmos so fascinating, yet the journey inward remains uninviting? How is it that we can navigate the stars and the abyss, yet struggle to navigate or quiet our own minds? What is the most basic and fundamental knowledge we should seek? What is the point of death, or more deeply, the purpose of suffering? Is there a *A TEXT MESSAGE WITH GOD* true and specific purpose for each person born into this world? If diversity is so beautiful, why has it also caused so much division and conflict? Why do people tend to see the worst in others first? Why is the question 'Why?' so powerful and often so loaded? What makes us perceive ourselves as so significant, as though we are the center of the universe? Why do some people always feel as if bad things are happening to them? Life follows the pattern of birth and death—what compels some to take the life of the innocent? Why do so many claim to know You (God), yet fail to know themselves? Why do so many deny the existence of Me?